Hearing Christ's Call

A Resource for the Formation and Spirituality of Catholic Men

Articles Based on Presentations Given at a Symposium for Ministry with Catholic Men

UNITED STATES CONFERENCE OF CATHOLIC BISHOPS
WASHINGTON, D.C.

The document *Hearing Christ's Call: A Resource for the Formation and Spirituality of Catholic Men* was developed by the Committee on Marriage and Family Life and the Committee on Evangelization of the United States Conference of Catholic Bishops (USCCB). It was reviewed by the committee chairmen, Bishop J. Kevin Boland and Bishop Michael W. Warfel, and has been authorized by the undersigned.

Msgr. William P. Fay
General Secretary
USCCB

Scripture texts used in this work are taken from the *New American Bible*, copyright © 1991, 1986, and 1970 by the Confraternity of Christian Doctrine, Washington, D.C. 20017 and are used by permission of the copyright owner. All rights reserved.

Unless noted, excerpts from *Vatican II: the Conciliar and Post Conciliar Documents, New Revised Edition*, edited by Austin Flannery, OP, copyright © 1996, Costello Publishing Company, Inc., Northport , N.Y., are used with permission of the publisher, all rights reserved. No part of these excerpts may be reproduced, stored in a retrieval system, or transmitted in any form or by any means—electronic, mechanical, photocopying, recording, or otherwise—without express written permission of Costello Publishing Company.

The presentations and speeches printed in this resource were given at a symposium on leadership for ministry with Catholic men, which was held on December 4-7, 2001, in Palm Beach, Florida.

For more information on the National Resource Center for Catholic Men, go to *www.nrccm.org*.

Cover art: © Massimo Listri/CORBIS
Photo credits: p. x Karen Callaway, *Northwest Indiana Catholic*/CNS; p. 4 Reuters/CNS; p. 6 Gregory L. Tracy, *The Pilot*/CNS; pp. 19, 32, 35, 42, 56, 70, 82 Human Issues Collaborative; p. 45 Tom Dermody, *Catholic Post*/CNS; p. 61 Debbie Hill/CNS; p. 77 United States Conference of Catholic Bishops; p. 86 Jim Whitmer.

First Printing, October 2002

ISBN 1-57455-503-0

Contents

Foreword

Since 1996, the emergence of a Catholic men's spirituality and how the Church in this country can nurture such a phenomenon have been topics of discussion and action for the U.S. Catholic bishops. They recognized in 1996 that Promise Keepers, a Christ-centered men's ministry movement, provided a "wakeup call to the Church to encourage and offer more ministry suited to the needs of [Catholic] men." This concern was brought to the forefront by the bishops' Committee on Marriage and Family Life, who in 1998 extended an invitation to the bishops' Committee on Evangelization to join in their efforts to nurture such a spirituality.

Since 1998, both committees have been addressing the cultivation of a Catholic men's spirituality. In September 1998, the bishops invited leadership from a variety of Catholic men's groups from across the country to the Center for Continuing Education at the University of St. Mary of the Lake in Mundelein, Illinois. The men who gathered represented a wide spectrum of groups, from large rallies to small parish-based groups. It was obvious to the committees' bishops that the Holy Spirit was very much alive in the witness they experienced at this first national gathering, and they felt that this gathering was a time for listening and learning from grass-roots leaders in Catholic men's ministries.

Three questions were put before those who gathered:
1. What are the various realities giving rise to a new interest in men's spirituality?
2. What responses are being offered in the Catholic community?
3. What are the leadership issues for bishops and for ministry leaders as they seek to promote an authentic Catholic men's movement?

The leaders emphasized consistently two points as they described their attempts to develop a specifically Catholic men's ministry: "First, [the leaders need to] incorporate what many Catholics find 'missing' in the Promise Keepers' experience, namely, sacramental celebration and devotion to the saints. Second, they urgently need resources and program materials particularly to use in the small groups."[1]

As the leaders reflected about the future in the "Introductory Report on Catholic Men's Ministries," they emphasized two things: "First, they identified the need for a national network of men's ministries and a central clearinghouse for information, leadership training, program resources, and general coordination among the many groups. Second, the lay leaders asked that their bishops and priests actively support men's ministries on diocesan and parish levels."

The report concluded by saying,

> For all who took part in the consultation it was a significant moment of listening and learning—and one for which we bishops are very grateful. Above all, we heard from the lay leaders a zeal for serving their brothers and a conviction that the evangelization of men is essential to the continuing renewal of the Church and the strengthening of families and society. There is a definite urgency about this work but, because it is still maturing, there is not yet a need to overly define or manage it. . . . At this point, Catholic men's ministry is a field open to cultivation by the Church's teachers and pastors. . . . We believe that the lay leaders with whom we gathered also heard [the bishops'] concerns about future directions for men's ministries. The Committee on Marriage and Family Life, with the collaboration of the Committee on Evangelization, plans to continue the dialogue with Catholic men's ministries.

In casual conversations among the participants, a dream began to emerge: the founding of the National Resource Center for Catholic Men. The dream became a reality at Mundelein, and the center was founded in Gaithersburg, Maryland, to provide training, recommend program materials, and offer assistance to leaders of men's ministry groups. The bishops established a liaison relationship with the center through committee staff.

In December 2001, the committees once again extended an invitation for Catholic men's leadership to join them for a symposium—this time to be held in North Palm Beach, Florida. Unlike the gathering in 1999, this gathering was more formational in direction, helping all those gathered to shape the future of Catholic men's ministries across the country. Once again, it was obvious that the Holy Spirit was very much alive in those who gathered. The bishops, who served as chairmen, welcomed the participants enthusiastically and joined members of their committees throughout the symposium.

The committees have kept their brother bishops informed through regular reports on the development of Catholic men's ministries. In May 2002, the committee chairmen reported to their brother bishops in "A Progress Report on Catholic Men's Ministries," which was also sent to all those who participated in the 2001 symposium. In June 2002, committee staff wrote to the leaders of Catholic men's ministries and promised that the major addresses given at the symposium would be compiled. *Hearing Christ's Call: A Resource for the Formation and Spirituality of Catholic Men* contains not only the presentations but other resources as well.

Hearing Christ's Call provides leaders of Catholic men's groups with presentations on key themes in the spiritual formation of men. It is one way our bishops are meeting the challenge given at the first gathering in 1999—to provide resources for leaders in Catholic men's ministries.

We suggest the following topics for reflection as you read this book:

- **The Use of Sacred Scripture**: Understanding the place of the Bible in God's revelation and the proper use of it as a teacher and guide for Christian living
- **Inclusivity**: Welcoming men of different races, cultures, socioeconomic status, age, and so forth, as well as drawing upon different Catholic spiritual traditions, within a single, diverse ministry to Catholic men
- **Relationship with Women**: Engaging the meaning of equality and mutuality, as well as appreciating the gifts of women and being able to relate to women, with respect and genuine collaboration
- **Attending to the World of Work**: Helping men to integrate their faith in the workplace and to address specific situations therein from the standpoint of Catholic belief and social teaching

- **Attending to Family, Parish, and Society**: Assisting Catholic men in living as Christians in their homes and parishes and in contributing to the ongoing, evangelizing transformation of society

We are also happy to provide the following vision statement that was developed at the conclusion of the 2001 symposium. It provides some clear directives in the ongoing development of Catholic men's ministry.

It is our hope that *Hearing Christ's Call: A Resource for the Formation and Spirituality of Catholic Men* is the first of many Catholic resources to assist in the ongoing formation of Catholic men's ministry. ■

Rev. John E. Hurley, CSP
Executive Director
Secretariat for Evangelization

Dr. H. Richard McCord
Executive Director
Secretariat for Family, Laity,
Women, and Youth

NOTE

---

1. Committee on Marriage and Family Life and Committee on Evangelization, Unites States Conference of Catholic Bishops, "An Introductory Report on Catholic Men's Ministries" (July 1999). This introductory report and a subsequent progress report (2002) can be found on the website: www.usccb.org/laity/marriage.

A VISION STATEMENT FOR CATHOLIC MEN'S MINISTRY

We propose and commit to a vision of Catholic men's ministry that
- Fosters a spirituality in men that is Christ-centered and that moves men toward
  —Reconciliation
  —A loving relationship of mutuality with women
  —A Christian impact in the workplace
  —Ongoing conversion in oneself and the transformation of society
  —Brotherhood and friendship in Christ
  —Service in charity and justice
  —A consciousness of the history from which patriarchy has evolved

- Provides ongoing faith formation, for both leaders and participants, enabling them to share their personal encounters with Christ
- Nurtures the growth of Catholic identity in men in their many roles, for example, son, father, husband, worker, disciple, minister, and friend
- Encourages men to take responsibility for their faith formation
- Incorporates diverse and inclusive Catholic spiritual traditions, expressions, and practices that are sensitive to the ethnic and racial mix of Catholic men
- Takes into consideration spiritual needs and experiences that are particular to men

In order to accomplish this vision, the following general initiatives are needed:
- Involvement and support by bishops and pastors to encourage men's ministry and form its leadership
- Structures for dialogue and networking among all leaders in Catholic men's ministry
- Identification of existing resources and development of new ones for use in Catholic men's ministry at all levels
- Development of small groups for men at local levels, for example, in the parish and region

Developed by the participants of the Symposium on Leadership for Ministry with Catholic Men, December 2001

The Future Hope of Catholic Men's Ministries

BY BISHOP CARL K. MOEDDEL

It is appropriate—no, much more than appropriate, it is necessary—that we begin this symposium [on leadership for ministry with Catholic men] in prayer, invoking the guidance of the Holy Spirit. For I think that we can all acknowledge that we are here to do more than simply exchange our best thinking or our own convictions, or even to share our faith. We are here to get in touch with the movement of the Holy Spirit. We will do that in prayer and through each other, but we will need to be attentive throughout to the promptings of the Holy Spirit.

In this article I will attempt to provide the following: first, a brief and recent history of Catholic men's ministries in the United States; second, a reflection upon the last time some of us bishops met with some leadership of these ministries in 1998 at Mundelein and the outcomes of that meeting; third, a look at the present; and fourth, suggestions for some directions and values for the future journey.

The Brief and Recent History

It was probably in the last half of the decade of the 1980s that there appeared the first stirrings of what we would today call the Catholic men's spiritual movement. What Catholic men started to articulate at that time was a spiritual hunger: a desire to get in touch with their faith and their commitment to Jesus Christ, and to help each other to do that.

This took different forms in different places. In some areas, it seems to have grown out of the charismatic movement or the Cursillo or a specific parish spiritual

1

renewal program. In other areas, it seems to have come alive, triggered by or in reaction to Promise Keepers.

But the landscape of the Catholic Church in this country at that time did not seem conducive to, or does not explain, these beginnings. For they occurred at a time when Catholic fraternal organizations were struggling for their existence; when 80 to 85 percent of parish staffs were women and the involvement in the life of the Church reflected frequently a similar percentage; and when parish programs often focused on children and their religious education.

I am convinced that we can only look to the Holy Spirit to discover the reasons for the beginnings of this movement, which has taken on a variety of names but is, in substance, the same: a spirituality movement by and for Catholic men.

The Mundelein Consultation

In the 1990s, the bishops of the United States, through their national conference, began to look at this movement together, since many of them experienced it in their own dioceses. In 1998, these two committees of the bishops—that is, the Committee on Marriage and Family Life and the Committee on Evangelization—called together some bishops of these committees and some leadership of the movement from around the United States to discuss what was happening.

This fruitful and enjoyable discussion led to preliminary articulation of the needs for this movement and ministry from the leadership and also to reflection from the bishops. At that meeting, which took place in Chicago at Mundelein Seminary, some developments and trends were identified.

The leaders present identified needs for the movement, from their perspective. These included Catholic resources and materials for study and for small groups. They also identified leadership training as a need, as well as a broader, more visible, and more vocal support from bishops and parish priests. They also acknowledged that the movement needed to be marked by greater inclusivity of all Catholic men and that a broader range of spiritualities needed to be represented. And they expressed a desire to expand their own network and to develop a unifying structure or support system.

The bishops, for their part, offered thoughts for the reflection of the leaders. We also judged that the movement needed greater efforts at inclusivity and a broader range of spiritualities represented and presented. We further suggested reflection on the evolving roles of men and women, and cautioned against a simplistic, and perhaps even fundamentalistic, approach to the Sacred Scriptures.

A Look at the Present

Here, I will rely upon some personal reflections and observations as well as on the results of a 1999 survey conducted by Robert Otis.[1]

First, the Catholic men's spiritual movement appears to be alive and well in various different expressions throughout the country.

Second, some good things have happened as a result of the Mundelein consultation. Resources are being developed; networking is continuing; a National Resource Center for Catholic Men has been established.

Third, in 1999, the bishops of the United States received a report from our two hosting committees on Catholic men's ministry, which included a report on the Mundelein consultation.

The survey that I mentioned found some important commonalities among the various ministries in the United States. All of them focus on personal transformation and the transformation of society by sharing the Good News of Jesus Christ. All emphasize God's call to discipleship and living the Christian life. Some commonality can even be seen in the strategies used, since the majority use what Otis called the "funnel strategy": that is, meetings in large groups to feed participants into smaller, usually parish-based groups. The small groups are then supported by the larger or regional group.

All of the groups surveyed reported successes in responding to needs of Catholic men, but some also reported failures in garnering priest support or in attracting men, due to the busyness of their lives.

In this brief time, I am unable to do justice to describing the results of this survey or to drawing a picture of the present shape of this movement. So I will conclude this section with a quote from the summary of the survey, which amused me, probably because of the truth therein: "Connection to the Church is important. It appears that too close a relationship impedes getting things done while a relationship without support seriously hinders the viability of the ministry."

Some Direction and Values for the Future Journey
I personally want to encourage the present direction of this ministry—that is, toward small parish-based groups. For it is at the parish where our life as Church, as a community of faith, is lived out; and it is to the parish that Catholic men need to bring their talents and gifts to supporting that community and building the Kingdom of God. In addition, here are more of my hopes for men's ministry:
- To continue to encourage the move beyond personal conversion to include catechesis and adult faith formation
- To encourage a holistic and inclusive spirituality, or a variety of spiritualities whereby any Catholic man would find this movement enriching
- To continue to move from a focus inward, an introspective focus, to include and make room for a focus on outreach and doing the work of the Lord

I could make many more suggestions, but I think that to move beyond these at this time would be presumptive. Therefore, I will end these reflections by simply indicating that I personally am excited to watch the Holy Spirit at work in this movement and that I am willing to help in any way.

I look to the future with great hope, founded in the Spirit. May the Church continue to be enriched by the Catholic men's movements throughout our country. ∎

Bishop Carl K. Moeddel *is Auxiliary Bishop of the Archdiocese of Cincinnati. In addition to his service in Ohio, Bishop Moeddel serves on the United States Conference of Catholic Bishops' Committee on Marriage and Family Life and the Catholic Communication Campaign.*

SUGGESTED FURTHER READING FROM THE VATICAN AND BISHOPS' CONFERENCE

Vatican: *Christifideles Laici* (The Vocation and Mission of the Lay Faithful in the Church and in the World); *Tertio Millennio Adveniente* (On the Coming of the Third Millennium)

U.S. Catholic Bishops: *Because God Loves You*; *Called and Gifted: The American Laity*; *Called and Gifted for the Third Millennium*; *Catholic Household Blessings and Prayers*; *Gifts Unfolding: The Lay Vocation Today with Questions for Tomorrow*; *Go and Make Disciples: A National Plan and Strategy for Catholic Evangelization in the United States*; *Michael the Visitor* (video); *One Body: Different Gifts, Many Roles*; *States of Faith: A Look at Religion in America* (video); *Our Hearts Were Burning Within Us: A Pastoral Plan for Adult Faith Formation in the United States*

See p. 92 for ordering information.

NOTE

---

1. Robert Otis, DPM, "Survey Results of Regional Men's Ministries," unpublished survey (January 8, 1999).

The Major Building Blocks in Scripture for Men's Spirituality

BY REV. LAWRENCE BOADT, CSP

Catholic Spirituality and the Bible

Developing a specifically Catholic, masculine spirituality is not primarily the work of psychology nor of theology working separately and alone, but rather demands a subtle interplay of many modern social sciences (psychology, anthropology, sociology, and history) with the religious dimensions of the human, particularly Christian, and the even more narrowly defined ways of life and beliefs of the Catholic. For one to develop a balanced spirituality, it is critical first to forge the spiritual foundations of the *human being*—male *or* female, male *and* female—and then to establish the basis of spirituality in human community and interpersonal relationships, before exploring the specific strengths and needs of the male.[1] In the process of developing our spiritual models, we can indeed find major building blocks to work with in the Bible, but we will find far more general blocks applicable to men and women together than unique ones for men alone. Moreover, as we use the Bible as a resource, we will need to focus on the following important issues:

- The cultural distance between the Bible's time of composition and our present world
- The ways in which the Bible claims to be the definitive word of God, so that we do not become literalists in scriptural interpretation

7

- The Bible's assumed models of society and worldview (often expressed through its storytelling techniques), so we can avoid simplistic conclusions about defining the roles and rights of men and women today[2]

The Church's most recent authoritative directive on biblical studies, the 1993 Pontifical Biblical Commission's *On the Interpretation of the Bible in the Church* (which was issued on the centenary of *Providentissimus Deus* and the golden jubilee of *Divino Afflante Spiritu*, the two keystones of the Church's modern approach to the Bible), cautions us to adopt not a literalist or fundamentalist attitude to biblical texts, but an *ecclesial* one—one that proposes the truth of Scripture as it has been understood within the living community of the Church, alive and guided by the Holy Spirit.[3] Thus, in order to address the question "What is a masculine spirituality?", Catholics must commit to forging a pastoral response based on Scripture that is solidly ecclesial in the full sense of the word. This pastoral response must call males to recover and strengthen in their lives the full range of "Catholic" insights and instincts, including beliefs about the sacraments, the Church as institution, the commitment to social justice, and the life of grace; all these beliefs should be seen through the lens of Christ, who died and rose for all, established a Church, and summoned disciples to follow his way. Many strengths can be found in the widespread popularity of such male recovery movements as Promise Keepers, but Catholic men should also recognize the weaknesses of such movements when they do not presuppose nor demand the building of full ecclesial membership and commitment. Catholics are more than able to propose a sound male spirituality built on the biblical center that also maintains a very "Catholic" profile.

To propose such a male spirituality, we need to look to the Scriptures: What do they say? From whom do they come? To whom are they addressed? The answers are both obvious and often overlooked. The Scriptures are documents of a relationship. They express the mutual shared experience between God and the human family, but especially they take on this relationship by the community of Israel and the apostolic community. For example, if the youngest daughter in a family writes about the relationship of herself and her siblings with their parents, the story she writes is everyone's story, yet it is very much the special story of this daughter. The Scriptures talk about what we know of God, of what we know about human beings struggling to relate to God, and of how to act with regard to one another in light of knowing God. This message is the equivalent of St. Patrick's famous cloverleaf with three dimensions: God, God and us, and us and us. Note that I do not say "me" in this relationship. Sure, the Scriptures talk a lot about individuals before God, but those stories are always told within the survival and fidelity of the whole community, as well as the position of that individual relative to the community. All biblical spirituality is then first and foremost addressed to the whole community as a way of life and integration, and only secondary is the call to each individual to embody this way fully in one's own personal dimension.[4]

The Key Pillars of the Old Testament: Faith and Spirituality

The Bible contains a broad collection of literary types, which may not seem to have much in common at times, but they all presuppose the same viewpoint about this divine-human relationship: God is unknowable unless God becomes a *self-revealing God*.[5] God has always taken the initiative to reveal himself to us; and because of this, what he has taught or made known about himself becomes conviction and eventually doctrine. We do not believe the Scriptures are normative just because someone defined them so, but we believe because of the inner essence of what they disclose. Because God is self-revealing, we encounter or meet or come to know the *real* God, even though only in a barely minimal way. And further, we believe that God revealed words, actual ideas, and meaning that our intellects could grasp, an understanding that goes beyond merely the memory of the personal experience of our individual self with God. This turns the fundamental relationship into a conversation between God and humanity, a privileged position of honor for the human, far above his or her proper level as a creature, by nature blind and silent before its creator. And if God permits a conversation of such near equality, then has not God established an even more profound relationship of partnership with human beings, in which we share in the divine plan, can talk of divine "moods" and "feelings" as though God were like us, and even speak of this unique relationship in metaphors of marriage or parenthood or other family images? And if this much is true, then we can take the relationship to the next step, which is very close to the heart of the Old Testament vision: we are most what God calls us to be when we imitate God in what we are and do. This is certainly the center of the Pentateuchal Torah in Leviticus 17-26—"Be holy, for I, the LORD, your God, am holy" (Lv 19:2)—and the ringing climax of creation in Genesis 1:26: "Let us make man in our image, after our likeness."

9

And, of course, this core spirituality of imitating God applies all the more to the New Testament declaration that Jesus is the son and we are called to follow him as disciples.

Finally, if we have arrived at this step, we can understand the central language of covenant for both testaments.[6] "I will take you as my own people, and you shall have me as your God" (Ex 6:7). The bond between God and Israel will not be broken by human misunderstanding or weakness or occasional failure in behavior. The sins and recalcitrance of individuals, even the vast majority of individuals, will not be sufficient to destroy the relationship, as long as some voices speak of it and hold it and proclaim it and call for conversion. Thus, the prophetic voice must continually speak of God's relationship lest we forget or let it die through silence or neglect.

All Judeo-Christian spirituality is built on these foundations:
- God gifts us with a relationship and knowledge of himself.
- This spirituality is a conversation and a dialogue of equals.
- This spirituality suggests God's unique bestowal of partnership, friendship, and even familial membership with us.
- This spirituality makes us recognize that we are made in God's image to imitate God and to be most fully our true selves.
- We are gathered in a covenant bond of love that will not be broken as long as we remember who this God is and can turn back to him.

The Pentateuch as the Primary Model for Biblical Spirituality
Building on these five pillars of the Old Testament understanding of God's relationship to humanity, we can also understand that Christians may claim justly the same belief—not just from faithful reading of the Hebrew scriptures, but from the Gospels—about Jesus the Christ, which reinforces each and every one of these points. Before moving on to the particular questions of a biblical spirituality for men, and so that we might be able to analyze the unfolding story of divine self-revelation in the Pentateuch as developing stages of the relationship, let us recap how the Pentateuch is the foundational blueprint of revelation for all men and women in Jewish tradition:
- Knowing God through delight in the goodness of Creation (Genesis)
- Discovering the name of God and listening to God's voice (Genesis)

- Trusting God as a God of deliverance in time of mortal danger (Exodus)
- Being made partners of God in the covenant experience (Exodus)
- Creating a priestly people in worshiping God (Leviticus)
- Becoming holy as God is holy in imitation of God (Leviticus)
- Learning prayer and prophetic mediation through Moses (Numbers)
- Recognizing God as our shepherd and companion in the desert (Numbers)
- Observing the law and commandments as a life-giving way (Deuteronomy)
- Conversing and sharing the joy in the divine word as friends (Deuteronomy)

In each of the five books of the Torah, the challenges of relationship and the responsibilities of spiritual growth on the part of Israel become more intense. No wonder we can call the Pentateuch the blueprint or constitution of Judeo-Christian spirituality.

Distinctive Male Characteristics

Much research has gone into studying the differences between men and women. From laboratory research to *Newsweek* to female spiritual writers such as Dolores Curran, there is general agreement that men display certain traits more naturally and more consistently than women do (and vice versa). For example, Patrick Arnold, in his book *Wildmen, Warriors and Kings*, suggests that primordial male traits include the following:

- Development of fighting skills to defend women and children
- The urge for hunting and food-gathering
- Competition for females between males
- Desire to stand up for order and truth
- Need to poke fun at or limit and bring down pomposity and power
- More interest in the outside world than in the home
- An intellectual approach to problems and a valuation of abstract thinking over sensitive feelings of awareness
- A desire for territory and space[7]

These traits can be supplemented by affirming that as a result male animals are basically loners by instinct, put so much importance on reproductive capability that they roam far from the home base, and conceive the connection to the inner life in terms of wilderness and independent survival. Furthermore, they are driven by the need to separate from the maternal womb and control of the home and are attracted by images such as the hero journey or arduous pilgrimage to the sacred sources. On the negative side,

- Male animals are usually wounded heroes from their fighting and competition who keep silent about their wounds.
- They are often stressed and on the edge of danger to themselves.
- They see suffering as part of their self-identity.
- They are often dependent on help but in most cases in danger of perishing from lack of help or resources along the journey.

David James, in his book *What Are They Saying About Masculine Spirituality*, identifies ten general masculine traits:

- Competitiveness
- Independence and autonomy
- Responsibility and accountability
- Linear thinking
- Provincial (territorial expansion) orientation
- Action orientation
- Production orientation
- Body-soul dualism (disconnect)
- Phallocentric orientation
- Evaluation of control and order[8]

James sees such traits as leading to a certain hardness and distance in men's orientations, a concern for concrete results, a special satisfaction in successful accomplishment of goals, and an outward focus.

Joseph Martos and Richard Rohr talk about the male gifts of mind, form, and speech—that is, of logic, language, organization, and order (while women are characterized by meditation, memory, and song—that is, creativity, intuition, synthesis, relationship, and affectivity).[9] They also talk about the Western ideal of masculinity that emphasizes toughness, independence, capability, and a can-do attitude. No one possesses him, but he possesses women; emotions are fine as long as they don't get in the way of what is right and logical.

Sam Keen, in his book *Fire in the Belly*, notes that males picture themselves performing certain societal roles and therefore gravitate to these images, which are distinct from what they conceive to belong to the feminine:

- The hunter
- The planter
- The warrior
- The Dionysius figure
- The prophet
- The powerful person
- The image of God
- The scientific man
- The self-made man
- The self-measuring man[10]

But Keen also notes that men greatly value the life of virtue, and he names ten heroic virtues that stand highest in male estimation:

- The virtue of wonder
- The virtue of empathy
- The virtue of heartful mind
- The virtue of moral outrage
- The virtue of right livelihood
- The virtue of enjoyment
- The virtue of friendship
- The virtue of communion
- The virtue of husbanding
- The virtue of wildness

The valuation of such roles and virtues leads men to look for exemplars and models to follow.

Enough said. The individual items on these lists all need fuller explanations by their authors than is given here. But it is clear that certain traits of the male recur on every list, and in a real sense, all these lists stand in fundamental agreement on the basic description of what are distinctive male qualities.[11]

Masculine Obstacles to Overcome

We need to go one step further and note that all these authors also propose that men have obstacles and difficulties to overcome if they are to handle the negative aspects of masculinity maturely and in a healthy manner. Thus Keen outlines another ten key areas in which most men need to grow:

- Moving from sunny pragmatism to a darker wisdom of the unconscious
- Dropping knowledge of all the answers to living out the question
- Abandoning cocksureness to accept doubt
- Overcoming numbness to express manly grief
- Replacing artificial toughness with a virile fear
- Releasing shame and guilt by accepting responsible morality
- Escaping isolation by accepting awareness of loneliness
- Going from false optimism to honest moments of despair
- Letting go of compulsive action to just waiting
- Embracing renewal and rebirth[12]

Philip Culbertson, in his book *The New Adam: The Future of Male Spirituality*, sees twelve stumbling blocks for men that must be overcome:

- The identification of God as father
- The fear of the feminine
- The suppression of a broad range of human emotions
- The valuation of self-sufficiency
- The misunderstanding of reciprocal relationships
- The insistence that "doing" is more manly than "being"
- The problem of not knowing who he is when not in charge
- The heritage of body-soul dualism and dismissal of sexuality and body
- The need to control and the fear of chaos and spontaneity
- The assumption that incompleteness or unpredictability is failure
- Preference for linearity over circularity, conditioned by the male anatomy
- Domination by men in the Church of all spiritual directions and theologies[13]

We can add also the observations of Aaron Kipnis, who lists in his book *Knights Without Armor* the tasks men need to undertake to find their souls healed:

- To admit their woundedness
- To begin the healing process by examining their wounds

- To rebuild self-esteem on deep masculine foundations
- To break out of old stereotypes and allow for diversity
- To reclaim the ancient, sacred images of masculinity
- To apply the myths of the masculine soul to daily living
- To rediscover the rites of male initiation
- To heal the wounds between fathers and sons
- To learn to love and work in ways that heal masculine life
- To restore connections to the ancestors and accept mortality
- To build male community
- To heal the wounds between the sexes
- To develop a male-affirming psychology[14]

Jed Diamond, in his book *The Warrior's Journey Home: Healing Men, Healing the Planet*, offers a similar set of healing models:
- Balance the desire *to do* with the desire *to be*
- Understand and heal the confusion between sex and love
- Transform ambivalent feelings toward women and children
- Express grief over the absence of the father
- Risk getting close to other men
- Change self-hatred to self-actualization
- Acknowledge the wounds of body and soul
- Uncover the basic roots of our insecurity
- Acknowledge and heal childhood abuse
- Explore the causes of violence, and change destructive behaviors
- Return to the spirit of true warriors[15]

Archetypal Images and Male Spirituality

Much of what has been written, particularly about male traits and characteristics and the need for men to overcome their "woundedness" and be healed, is driven by the current fascination with the Jungian archetypes. Carl Jung has defined these archetypes as blueprints for the male potential of becoming the mature, masculine person that lies deep in the unconscious. They are primordial images of the masculine "self."[16] At a person's center, this self pulls together and reconciles all the dynamic psychological opposites in our psyches. The recognition of the primary archetypes enables us to integrate conflicting or opposite psychological strands into a larger whole, a vision if you will, that gives us new insight to change our behaviors and identities, and to live a new meaning.[17]

Robert Moore and Douglas Gillette have written what has become almost a bible for writers on masculine identity and spirituality. In *King, Warrior, Magician, Lover* they define the four positive archetypes for men and their four dark opposites:

- The *king*, who is the wise and balanced leader
- The *shadow king*, who craves power and oppresses all others

- The *warrior*, who represents stamina, energy, focus, resolute behavior
- The *black knight*, who is egocentric, violent, and oppressive

- The *magician*, who is wise and prophetic
- The *evil sorcerer*, who manipulates spiritual authority

- The *lover*, who delights in and enjoys beauty, joy, and love
- The *addict*, who seeks all pleasure for the self at any cost[18]

These eight archetypes and anti-archetypes contain neatly most of the areas that the writers above have identified as specifically masculine. Each archetype has both strengths and weaknesses; and both psychology and religion seem to agree completely that a healthy person, not only in the world but also before God, must bring integration, reconciliation, and often healing to the two sides of each.

The most significant factor here for the task of developing a biblical spirituality addressed to males is understanding that these are *human* archetypes, and yet they also represent the most frequent and powerful images of *God* in the scriptures. It is not easy, therefore, to simply believe that the social and cultural values of the ancient world were deficient because they described the one God as male, and even more as a patriarchal God, embodying all of the limits of ancient social structures, families, and tribes. The primary images of God are not simply mirrors of the roles of tribal chieftain or father of the family, but have apparently emerged from the fundamental "hard-wiring" of the unconscious archetypes of masculine identity. If we are to assert that the Bible's understanding of God reflects primary archetypes of masculinity, we need to explore the actual biblical building blocks in given texts and the ways in which they are expressed literarily.

Although Moore, Gillette, and others use terms such as "king" and "warrior" that *seem* to reflect biblical language, we need to question this before assuming it. First, because of their Christian background, these writers are already influenced by biblical language and imagery in choosing their terms for the archetypes, and so may actually narrow the real psychological dimensions in the soul to preconceived categories or descriptions. Second, the Bible does not record careful sociological and anthropological scientific data, but expresses through artistic literary drama and diverse literary types a God of *relationship* that defies any narrow definition or any adequate human terminology. It is my personal opinion that the Bible often contradicts and counters stereotypes of "warrior," "king," and "magician" with an expansive view that summons men past merely natural archetypes or images of the self to a higher, more spiritual vision of the self that would be inclusive of men and women before God, or perhaps better, together in God's image and likeness (Gn 1:26).[19]

The Scriptures and Stages of a Man's Life

From Erik Erikson to Lawrence Kohlberg to Gail Sheehy, the stages of development from childhood to old age have been chronicled and dissected in a variety of discrete steps and plateaus.[20] In his play *As You Like It*, William Shakespeare spoke of the seven ages of a man's life. Erikson has eight stages. Sheehy stressed the key stages of adult growth: intimacy, generativity, and the search for integrity, which occur during our twenties and forties. For our purposes, we can note that those who outline the characteristics of the male and masculine spirituality almost always assume such stages of development. Much of the impulse has come from Freud's theories about psychological development and the unconscious.[21] Stages such as separation of the child from the womb, the finding of identity apart from different-gender parents, and the discovery of independence outside the home are all commonly recognized. Most important for the male is the moment when he must separate from the mother and the feminine control of the home to become an adult male. Doing it alone, the man runs the risk of either suppressing most feminine qualities and over-developing the non-integrated dark side of his masculine archetypes—or else clinging to the feminine security he has known and failing to become an autonomous, mature male.

Most of the foregoing authors stress certain important aspects of passing through these stages that will have much relevance to the biblical view of healthy spirituality.

These aspects include (1) the pain of letting go of the previous stage and the feeling of wrenching free in the hope and expectation of a different experience; (2) the importance for rites and initiations to lead us from one stage to the next because we are part of a community that must recognize the change; (3) the need for wise mentors and teachers who can help us learn the wisdom and truths of the new stages of our life in order that we might succeed and also be recognized more fully as a respected adult in the community; and (4) the recognition of our woundedness—or perhaps better, our mortality—that we might discover our need for God. While some of these aspects are important "on the way up" in life, this last one is "part of the way down" towards weakened older age. While life may be described in stages, it can also be described effectively as a journey in which we spend much of our time on the way towards more control and empowerment and achievement, but then must be matched by a parallel learning of the virtues on the way down: wisdom, respect, leadership, judgment, forgiveness, compassion, and generosity.

If we conceive the language of life stages in this way, we will have little trouble building a bridge to the Bible as a major resource for defining the masculine journey in life. We might note here too that the New Testament seems to be permeated with references to knowing Christ and finding one's stages of life marked by sacramental actions of Baptism and the Eucharist, and identifying Jesus' own life journey as a passage of water and blood, representing our participation in him and his saving event by means of the sacraments.[22] Thus, instead of being primarily for women, sacraments should appeal strongly to males and perhaps need to be re-languaged to give men more involvement in sacramental life as part of their male journey.

The Question of Fatherhood

Another theme that recurs frequently in the discussion of male distinctiveness and of subsequent male problems in achieving mature development is that of the role of fatherhood. Many boys experience poor relationships in conflict with their fathers, feel the emptiness of an absent father, or even suffer from an abusive father. Even in relatively stable homes, many fathers are unable to express their emotions or feelings with their sons or even to communicate their life experiences to their son. Since everyone agrees that the man-to-man relationship between father and son is critical throughout the stages of childhood and adolescence, many adult men live with a gaping lacuna at their center—a desire for a father that would be both the hero and model to emulate, and at the same time the confidant, friend, and guide. If the boy is to value his identity as a member of a family and community, the approval of the father is important in making the major transitions to new stages.[23]

The most detailed study of the question of fatherhood in the Bible and its relationship to the issues raised by psychologists is John Miller's *Calling God "Father,"* in which Miller argues that the Bible puts great stress on God as a fatherly male deity in the Old Testament and specifically as "Father" in the New because the Israelite faith tradition recognized instinctively that women understood their motherly role more naturally because of the close bond between mother and child, but men did not because of their marginality to the reproductive process.[24]

Fatherhood is a cultural acquisition that must be learned and therefore taught. If the culture and beliefs do not support the father's involvement with his children and his society, then men will spin away from responsible roles in family and moral leadership. Miller says that the importance of God as father can not be underestimated. No father exists apart from God's fatherhood, and human fathers share in the divine fatherhood. For Miller, the Bible clearly recognizes God as neither male nor female, without male anatomy nor limited to male imagery. Instead, the Bible sees that the masculine attributes and idea of fatherhood express a deeper relationship to the world, one that is committed to being present to it; active, alert, and compassionate toward its inhabitants; and not withdrawn or passive, that is, merely a part of it. Drawing on the general attributes of the masculine as distinct from the feminine, biblical tradition affirmed a God transcendent to the world but proactive towards it.

If we accept Miller's line of reasoning, then the efforts to discover major biblical building blocks for a masculine spirituality become much easier. We do not have to approach the question through arguments for and against the cultural presuppositions of ancient societies that deprived women of their identity and integrity, but we can define a positive effort to establish an intimate relationship of God to the world that would respect both parties as independent and willing, and not as one coercing the other. In this sense, the affirmation of the male language actually serves to reinforce a view of God that is more often associated with the feminine qualities of caring and intimacy.

Biblical Spirituality and Life Journeys

It is time to return to the question of defining the major building blocks of Scripture that we might apply to developing a healthy male spirituality. Building on the key insights of the Old Testament that affirm how humans are involved in a unique and highly graced divine-human relationship, we can ask, "What are the primary means by which specifically male needs and interests are addressed in the Bible to achieve that relationship?" Interestingly, most of the historical narratives—and also most of the action stories—use imagery we have identified with the key characteristics of men. We can outline a few.

The Hero Journey

1. The primeval myth that emphasizes the arduous journey from one space to another and back to the beginning again: for example, Adam and Eve expelled from the garden (Gn 3); Cain expelled to the East (Gn 4); Noah set upon the waves to Armenia (Gn 6-8); Abraham's ancestors leaving Ur for Harran (Gn 11).

2. The ancestors' call to leave their homes and go to a foreign land where they will encounter God and receive revelation and a new promise: for example, the journeys of Abraham (Gn 12, 15), Jacob (Gn 28), and Joseph (Gn 37). (Note that none of these heroes actually understand their call or revelation at the time.) Their success is an internal journey of the spirit to obedience to God and the identifying of their will with the divine leader as father to them. This identification becomes powerful in the story of Isaac's sacrifice for Abraham (Gn 22), the late-night struggle with an angel for Jacob (Gn 32:22-32), and the insights expressed by Joseph (Gn 45:4-8, 50:19-21).

3. The great exodus journey of tribulation from Egypt through the desert to the new land, which is the core story of biblical faith and which occupies four full books of the Pentateuch (Exodus to Deuteronomy).

4. The exile and return of Judah as a new exodus journey in the message of Isaiah 40-55.

5. The interpretation of Jesus' death and resurrection as a new exodus journey by St. Paul in Romans 6:1-3 and 1 Corinthians 10:1-5.

Conquest Journey

1. The story of the conquest of the land in Joshua, Judges, and the Books of Samuel, in which the asceticism, discipline, and obedience of Israel are interspersed with the heroic deeds of individual heroes such as Samson, Joshua, Caleb, and Samuel himself.

2. The idealization of the Davidic monarchy, and especially of David himself as king, warrior, trickster, and lover all at once (1 Sm 16 to 2 Sm 20). David's great friendship and loyalty to God is matched by his woundedness. He is not

an unalloyed hero, but is crafted and portrayed as the author of the Psalms—
with their rich mixture of pathos, suffering, failure, need, loyalty, praise, vic-
tory, and hope, all rolled into one.[25]

3. The divine warrior tradition also plays a significant role: it is God alone who
    is the Lord of Armies that makes accomplishments possible and grants suc-
    cesses.[26] The key passage is the song of Moses in Exodus 15, but the divine
    warrior tradition also permeates the mythology and ancient remembrances of
    God in the plague tradition (Ex 5-12); the historical narratives (Jgs 4-5); the
    prophetic texts, especially those against foreign powers (Is 13-23; Jer 46-51;
    Ez 25-32; Ob); exilic reflections (Hb 3; Zec 14; Ez 38-39); and the Psalms
    (Ps 18, 23, 68, 74, 89, 91, 110, 136, and many others).

4. The Book of Revelation in the New Testament is perhaps the strongest and
    most thorough picture of God as divine warrior in battle against the kingdom
    of Satan. It draws heavily on the Old Testament language of Daniel, Ezekiel,
    Zechariah, and the book of Psalms (278 of its 404 verses echo older biblical
    texts). In this rich tapestry of images, God is not only the giver of victory and
    fighter for justice and right, but the compassionate one, the protector of the
    weak, the bestower of peace and prosperity, the wounded lamb that now lives
    victoriously, and the benign ruler that claims the loyalty of all peoples. It is a
    veritable workbook on how God can integrate all the male characteristics in
    one model.[27]

Discipleship

1. The New Testament model for followers of Jesus is above all that of the *disciple*.
    Jesus calls the individual to his side to learn about relationship, sends the per-
    son to perform and proclaim what he has learned, needs the disciple's support
    in his suffering, and bestows on him his own status and commission when he
    departs.

2. St. Paul, above all, represents this disciple set apart from the others and
    drawn clearly and sharply for our imitation. Paul himself embodies the full
    range of male characteristics of strength and weakness. He recognizes them
    realistically and re-integrates his life and its purpose in Christ. He, in turn, is
    a mentor for each of his disciples to pass through their stages of following

Christ. Many scholars wonder about the authenticity of the pastoral epistles, but if we look at the New Testament as a conscious creation of the early Church to mirror what true discipleship is, then it is truly astounding that these later letters represent the moment of the full integration of Paul's teaching and the coming to adulthood of his communities at the end of his ministry.[28] Paul guides successfully the infant Church to its next stage of mature life.

The Bible as a Story of the Adult Spiritual Journey

The scriptural story of the Old Testament in particular is constructed in collections of books that emphasize certain widely recognized themes. These include the centrality of worship, especially connected to the Sabbath and the seasons of the year: Passover, Pentecost, and Succoth; the importance of the land, especially the land of the ancestors and the promised land (which turn out to be the same); and the temple as the dwelling place of God that brings blessing to the land. These themes are interwoven through most books of the Hebrew scriptures, not merely in a static manner, but interestingly in a tension between going towards and going away; between conquest and exile; between faithfulness to and unfaithfulness against. The journey motifs we have just examined play a vital role in structuring the perceived relationship between God and Israel as one that is not bound to one place, but is universal; is not constant, but must be lost and regained in practice; and is sometimes close, but sometimes alienated. In theological terms, it is the story of sin and grace. In accordance with ancient ways of thinking, these poles reflect the opposing tensions played out between God and humanity; between sacred precinct and ordinary space and time; between the holy and the profane. This is the way of reconciling and explaining the extraordinary interaction between the divine and the merely human; between creator and creature; between the Holy One and Israel—that the unique revelation of Scripture proclaimed.

Pilgrimage

Above we examined the theme of the hero journey as an archetype of the male spiritual journey. Another variation on this is the pilgrimage. While all people can make a pilgrimage, some aspects were clearly intended as a task for men rather than women.[29] The usual steps of pilgrimage, like those of the hero journey, include the following:

- The desire to go to a place of sacredness to gain new insight or a special gift
- The separation from the ordinary and from home, leaving much behind
- The arduous journey against many obstacles and threats to reach the goal
- A purification or testing at the goal in order to receive the knowledge or prize
- A sacred experience after entering the sanctuary
- The return journey home, which includes overcoming more obstacles
- Homecoming and integration back into society but with the prize in hand
- Help, healing, or empowerment for those to whom the pilgrim gives the prize

Scripture can be read as reflecting this kind of journey for men. Different parts of the Old Testament emphasize different key themes:
- Leaving home for a new life after overcoming obstacles (Abraham in Genesis)
- Risking danger to journey to freedom (Exodus)
- Building a desert sanctuary and meeting the divine (Leviticus)
- Reaching a new land and overcoming obstacles (Numbers)
- Establishing a new relationship of trust and obedience (Deuteronomy)
- Conquering and transforming society (the historical books: Judges and Kings)
- Being sent forth to carry the divine word to others (Prophets)
- Depending on God's strength and help on the way (Psalms)
- Enduring defeat and restoration to reach home again (exilic books)
- Bestowing the gift of peace and hope on others (Isaiah 2:1-4; 7:1-18)

On another level, the Pentateuch is often seen as a wilderness blueprint for Israel's subsequent life as a people in the land. The story opens in Genesis with the creation of the human couple as God's highest act of goodness, and then it follows that couple as it becomes Israel. But the story has a particular point to make. The couple is created in the divine image with the freedom to choose and the understanding of good and evil. Free will and divine purpose both work at the same time, sometimes together, and often at cross-purposes. The two key areas of the ideal cooperation are procreation and governance of the world, both exercised as vice-regents for God's own role as father, creator, king, and teacher. Indeed, the Pentateuch can readily be interpreted as the story of how humans are called to learn how to be good at their jobs. The heavy emphasis on such strong male images, as Miller would say, underscores the need to teach the men, above all, how to be responsible in their roles in society. Let us note here that the five books of Moses indeed propose the key qualities of a masculine spirituality:

- Genesis 1-11 shows how true fatherhood was perverted by men.
- Genesis 12-50 educates Israel on the roles of faithful but free sons.
- Exodus 1-18 calls on Israel to set off in courage to find freedom.
- Exodus 19-40 establishes strong bonds of friendship through worship.
- Leviticus 1-16 teaches purification and letting go of our possessions.
- Leviticus 17-27 demands justice, self-sacrifice, and moral effort.
- Numbers 1-20 describes the arduous desert journey of the people.
- Numbers 21-36 portrays Israel, the warrior, taking possession of the land.
- Deuteronomy 1-11 reaffirms Israel's special loving bond with God.
- Deuteronomy 12-34 marks lessons to be lived independently without Moses.

It might be noted that most of these major building blocks in the Pentateuch correspond roughly with elements of the archetypes that Moore and Gillette delineate:
- The *warrior* in Exodus and Numbers (and Joshua, Judges, and Samuel)
- The *king* in the creation accounts (e.g., Abraham and Moses)
- The *magician* in the Jacob and Moses stories
- The *lover* in creation (Ex 19-40, Dt)

The crucial point in mentioning these characteristics is that when talking about a biblical ideal of male spirituality, we will need to build the structure from the whole narrative, not just isolated stories or individual hero models. It is the interplay of elements in the entire Pentateuchal "story" that makes it possible to see how Scripture views the successes and failures of men as part of a growing and changing relationship with God. Scripture has an anchor or core in the fidelity of God's commitments and gives men hope and healing by the gracious forgiveness and consistent compassion of a divine friend.[30]

Jesus as a Model

Up to this point, I have concentrated primarily on the vast canvas of the Old Testament "story" (which of course is much more than a story or narrative; it is a rich mixture of poem, wisdom, oracle, song, law, and moral exhortation), but the same points can be drawn as sharply for the New Testament proclamation of Jesus in the Gospel. The two key historical narratives of the New Testament are both journey stories: the Gospels as the journey of Jesus, and Acts as the journey of the early Church. Many of the themes of leaving home, undergoing testing and rejection, accepting the divine encounter of the cross, passing through the

SOME CONCRETE STEPS FOR THE
BIBLICAL EDUCATION OF MEN

If we are to incorporate the Bible into the Christian education of men as faithful members of the Church, we must challenge men to acknowledge that they are spiritual beings and hunger for a deeper knowledge of the way or journey to God that they must undertake. This could be taught using these ongoing methods:

- Men's planning groups for undertaking missions of the local church
- The highlighting of initiation rites and marking of transitions and achievements for men
- The identifying of men as the teachers and mentors of youth
- Family support ministry that includes sustaining and healing families
- The involvement of men in the planning and organizing of outreach ministries to the city
- The reforming of structures that are run by and dominated by women
- Homilies, talks, and preaching on responsible male leadership qualities

barrier of death, and returning alive and in glory mirror the classic hero and pilgrim archetypal journeys. Using these male models, we might note the following qualities that identify Jesus as the successful male par excellence:[31]

- Showed constant detachment and inner freedom as an individual
- Was willing to undergo suffering for others out of love
- Became a shaman and healer in the true *magician* mode
- Aware constantly of his relationship with God and God's spirit
- Challenged accepted stereotypes and broke from them
- Dealt with men and women equally
- Understood a healthy father-son relationship
- Confronted death without hesitation and endured it as a warrior
- Used the humor and irony of the *trickster* to deflate pomposity
- Established a kingdom of justice, benignity, and inclusivity

With these qualities, Jesus asks a rigor and loyalty of disciples to learn from the master; he offers them both instruction and independence to carry out his way;

he is not afraid to expect from them the same virtues of courage and strength before persecution and martyrdom; he asks them to accept the mature adulthood of inner understanding and faith that he had; and he expects them to mentor and pass this on to new generations.

St. Paul would often repeat in his letters the commands of Jesus to his disciples: insisting we put on the armor of Christ (Eph 6:7-10; Col 3:7-9; Phil 3:12-15), seeing ourselves as sent to be ministers from God (Rom 1:1-6; 2 Cor 4-5; 2 Tm 4:1-4), imitating Christ (1 Cor 4:16; Eph 5:1; 1 Thes 1:6), among others.

Once again such sketchy examples suggest that it is not simply imitating Jesus or Paul that is proposed by the New Testament, but rather embarking on the journey that their stories set for us: men need to envision the Gospels as sketches or complex models for male energy to embrace, undertake, and make its own. They are invited to read the epistles of Paul as the lessons in becoming one with Christ, to try to initiate the same number of elements into their own life journeys, and to integrate such qualities and embody them more deeply.

Individual Biblical Models
For homiletic purposes or for encouraging specific elements of masculine spiritual growth, we might turn to the story of individual biblical men. Arnold, in his *Wildmen, Warriors and Kings*, develops effectively models of Abraham around pilgrimage and wise patriarch themes; models of Moses as warrior and also healing magician; models of Solomon as king; models of Elijah as wild man; models of Elisha as healer; models of Jeremiah as truth-teller and bearer of honesty; models of Jonah as trickster (where the ironies of his story convey the mysterious action of God); and sometimes models of Solomon in the Song of Songs, those who keep the covenant in Exodus and Deuteronomy, and vague people who are upright as lovers.[32]

Since developing individual biblical models would require the space of another article, we can simply note their possibility as a further line of exploration, since the main point to be made is that these individual figures must not be seen as providing *by themselves* an adequate picture of integrated masculine spirituality in the biblical view. Each needs the others. And they all must be read as part of the larger *relationship* of God and Israel as heard and remembered in their stories—whether all of the Old Testament, just the Pentateuch, or perhaps the New Testament alone. ∎

Rev. Lawrence Boadt, CSP, *is President and Publisher of Paulist Press. He holds a doctorate in Sacred Scripture from the Pontifical Biblical Institute in Rome.*

SUGGESTED FURTHER READING FROM THE VATICAN AND BISHOPS' CONFERENCE

Vatican: *Veritatis Splendor* (*The Splendor of Truth*), *Dei Verbum* (*Dogmatic Constitution on Divine Revelation*)

U.S. Catholic Bishops: *Family Ministry: A Pastoral Plan and a Reaffirmation*; *Follow the Way of Love: A Pastoral Message of the U.S. Catholic Bishops to Families*; *Putting Children and Families First: A Challenge for Our Church, Nation, and World*

See p. 92 for ordering information.

NOTES

1. See Lawrence Cunningham and Keith Egan, *Christian Spirituality: Themes from the Tradition* (Mahwah, N.J.: Paulist Press, 1996); Michael Downey, *Understanding Christian Spirituality* (Mahwah, N.J.: Paulist Press, 1997). Both books explore the role of Scripture and its major themes in the history of Christian spirituality.

2. Carroll Stuhlmueller's *New Paths Through the Old Testament* (Mahwah, N.J.: Paulist Press, 1989) offers several suggestions for understanding and reading the Bible as a whole. Margaret Nutting Ralph's *And God Said What?*, rev. ed. (Mahwah, N.J.: Paulist Press, 2002), is the best introduction to the art of understanding literary forms in interpreting scriptural stories.

3. Pontifical Biblical Commission, *On the Interpretation of the Bible in the Church* (Boston: St. Paul Books and Media, 1994).

4. See Antony Campbell, SJ, *God First Loved Us: The Challenge of Accepting Unconditional Love* (Mahwah, N.J.: Paulist Press, 2000). He treats the nature of revelation as God's initiative to the world and as present in all levels of the Scriptures with its application for Christian life.

5. See Karl Rahner, SJ, and Cardinal Joseph Ratzinger, *Revelation and Tradition* (New York: Herder & Herder, 1966); Cardinal Joseph Ratzinger, Alois Grillmeier, and B. Rigaud, "Dogmatic Constitution on Divine Revelation," in *Commentary on the Documents of Vatican II*, vol. III, ed. Herbert Vorgrimler (New York: Herder & Herder, 1968); John L. McKenzie, "Aspects of Old Testament Thought," in *New Jerome Biblical Commentary* (Englewood Cliffs, N.J.: Prentice Hall, 1990), nos. 103-110; Raymond Collins, "Inspiration," in *New Jerome Biblical Commentary*, no. 65.

6. See Roland J. Faley, *Bonding with God: A Reflective Study of Biblical Covenant* (Mahwah, N.J.: Paulist Press, 1997).

7. Patrick Arnold, *Wildmen, Warriors and Kings: Masculine Spirituality and the Bible* (New York: Crossroad, 1991), 29-50.

8. David C. James, *What Are They Saying About Masculine Spirituality?* (Mahwah, N.J.: Paulist Press, 1996), 42-43.

9. Richard Rohr and Joseph Martos, *The Wild Man's Journey: Reflections on Male Spirituality*, rev. ed. (Cincinnati, Ohio: St. Anthony Messenger Press, 1996).

10. Sam Keen, *Fire in the Belly: On Being a Man Today* (New York: Bantam, 1991).

11. See also John Sanford and George Lough, *What Men Are Like* (Mahwah, N.J.: Paulist Press, 1988); Philip Culbertson, *The New Adam: The Future of Male Spirituality* (Minneapolis: Fortress Press, 1992); James B. Nelson, *The Intimate Connection: Male Sexuality, Masculine Spirituality* (Philadelphia: Westminster Press, 1988); James Dittes, *The Male Predicament: On Being a Man Today* (San Francisco: Harper & Row, 1985).

12. Keen, *Fire in the Belly*, 125-151.

13. Culbertson, *The New Adam*, 111; see James, *Masculine Spirituality*, 25-26.

14. Aaron Kipnis, *Knights Without Armor: A Practical Guide for Men in Quest of Masculine Soul* (New York: Tarcher/Pedigree, 1991), vii-x.

15. Jed Diamond, *The Warrior's Journey: Healing Men, Healing the Planet* (Oakland, Calif.: New Harbingers Publications, 1994), 2.

16. See Carl Jung, *The Undiscovered Self* (New York: New American Library, 1957).

17. See Carl Jung, *Man and His Symbols* (New York: Doubleday, 1964).

18. Robert Moore and Douglas Gillette, *King, Warrior, Magician, Lover: Rediscovering the Archetypes of the Mature Masculine* (San Francisco: Harper & Row, 1990), 44-62.

19. See Kenneth Leech, *Soul Friend: The Practice of Christian Spirituality* (San Francisco: Harper & Row, 1977); Matthew Linn, Sheila Fabricant Linn, and Dennis Linn, *Good Goats: Healing Our Image of God* (Mahwah, N.J.: Paulist Press, 1993).

20. See Erik Erikson, *Childhood and Society* (New York: W. W. Norton, 1950); Lawrence Kohlberg, *Essays on Moral Development: The Philosophy of Moral Development* (San Francisco: Harper & Row, 1981); and Gail Sheehy, *Passages* (New York: Dutton, 1976), 10-19.

21. Sigmund Freud, in *Moses and Monotheism* (New York: Alfred A. Knopf, 1939), applies much of his psychoanalytical theory to the development of Judeo-Christian religion.

22. See Matthew 28:16-20; John 19:34-35; Romans 6:1-3; 1 Corinthians 10:1-4, 11:23-32; 1 Peter 1:22-25; and 1 John 4-5. For the heavily sacramental emphasis in John's Gospel, see Bruno Barnhart, *The Good Wine: Reading John from the Center* (Mahwah, N.J.: Paulist Press, 1993), 57-62, 373-377.

23. See David Blankenhorn, *Fatherless America: Confronting Our Most Urgent Social Problem* (New York: Basic Books, 1995); David Popenoe, *Life Without Father: Compelling New Evidence that Fatherhood and Marriage are Indispensable for the Good of Children and Society* (New York: The Free Press, 1996).

24. John W. Miller, *Calling God "Father": Essays on the Bible, Fatherhood and Culture* (Mahwah, N.J.: Paulist Press, 1999).

25. See Klaus Seybold, *Introducing the Psalms* (Edinbugh: T & T Clark, 1990), 34-39.

26. See Patrick D. Miller, "God the Warrior: A Problem in Biblical Interpretation and Apologetics," in *Israelite Religion and Biblical Theology: Collected Essays* (Sheffield, England: Sheffield Academic Press, 2000), 356-64; Frank M. Cross, "The Divine Warrior in Israel's Early Cult," in B. Altmann, ed., *Biblical Motifs* (Cambridge, Mass.: Harvard University Press, 1966), 11-30.

27. See Roland Faley, *Apocalypse Then and Now: A Companion to the Book of Revelation* (Mahwah, N.J.: Paulist Press, 1999). See also John J. Collins, *The Apocalyptic Imagination: An Introduction to the Jewish Matrix of Christianity* (New York: Crossroad Press, 1984).

28. See Mark Harding, *What Are They Saying About the Pastoral Epistles?* (Mahwah, N.J.: Paulist Press, 2001), for a full discussion concerning the relationship of Pauline authorship and Pauline legacy.

29. Victor Turner and Edith Turner, *Image and Pilgrimage in Christian Culture: Anthropological Perspectives* (New York: Columbia University Press, 1978); Jean Clift and Wallace Clift, *The Archetype of Pigrimage: Outer Action with Inner Meaning* (Mahwah, N.J.: Paulist Press, 1996).

30. This is not the only way to find male role models in the scriptures. A long tradition exists, that is based on the creation story of Adam and Eve that God is the friend of human beings, on the Abraham-Jacob cycle that God is a friend to the obedient patriarch, and on the David story of 2 Samuel for the king. But above all, it was Moses as the friend of God that was extolled (see, e.g., Sir 45:1-5).

31. See John O' Grady, *Models of Jesus Revisited* (Mahwah, N.J.: Paulist Press, 1994).

32. See Arnold, *Wildmen, Warriors and Kings*, footnote 7, for detailed descriptions of Old Testament figures as male models.

Men in Family Life: The Question of Headship Re-Examined

BY DR. JAMES HEALY

Since 1988 I have been involved in Catholic men's ministry, and I believe I have seen two movements within it. The first was a tremendous rediscovery of unity among Christians: a new realization among Christian men that our wells were connected by a deep underground source, Jesus Christ—his mission, identity, and teachings.

The second movement, while retaining an underlying sense of unity, also identifies and affirms what is distinctive about our Catholic identity. This combination of "What makes us the same?" and "What makes us different?" is an essential part of our human experience. It is this blending of our sameness and our uniqueness that makes us who we are, whether as a person, as a family, as a country, or as Catholics. This article is a contribution to the second movement.

Headship in Marriage

As Catholic men try to bring men's ministry more squarely into the Catholic experience, one area of turbulence—probably the area of greatest turbulence within my field of family ministry—has been the question of leadership in marriage. Certainly, one major effect of men's ministry has been to call men to greater involvement in and commitment to their marriages and their responsibilities as fathers, and I praise God for this movement of the spirit. Where the tension comes from is in how we understand the relationship between husbands and wives regarding authority. While many men espouse what has come to be called mutuality and equal authority in marriage, others in men's ministry believe in what is generally called "headship." It is difficult in the space of this article to do justice to the nuances that men have offered regarding "biblical headship," but let me attempt a basic definition: headship means that in relation to his wife, the husband is called by God to provide the spiritual leadership and to have the final say, when necessary, in decision making. Further, it is the responsibility of the wife to accept and respond to this leadership role of the husband. Feelings run high in this area, both for men and for women, and I suspect that this issue, more than any other, has so far kept men's ministry from being more fully welcomed into the Catholic Church.

Church Teaching on Marriage

I believe the greatest contribution I can make to this discussion is to reflect on official church teaching. Although there are many ways of dealing with this subject, I will largely confine myself to what several popes have taught and to other authoritative documents from Rome since Vatican II. I will attempt a few comments of my own, but my primary intent is to look squarely at the teachings that have been offered to us.

It would be fair to say that before the Second Vatican Council, official pronouncements on the relationship between men and women in marriage emphasized the man's headship and the woman's submission. For example, in 1880, Pope Leo XIII (1878–1903) wrote the following in his encyclical *On Christian Marriage* (*Arcanum divinae Sapientiae*):

> The husband is the chief of the family and the head of the wife. The woman, because she is flesh of his flesh and bone of his bone, must be subject to her husband and obey him; not indeed, as a servant, but as a companion, so that her obedience shall be wanting in neither honor nor dignity. Since the husband represents Christ, and since the wife represents the Church, let there always be, both in him who commands and in her who obeys, a heaven-born love guiding both in their respective duties. For "the husband is the head of the wife, as Christ is the head of the Church. . . . Therefore, as the Church is subject to Christ, so also let wives be to their husbands in all things." (no. 11)

Fifty years later, in 1930, Pope Pius XI (1922–1939) in his own *On Christian Marriage* (*Casti Connubii*) approvingly quoted the above statement from his predecessor. He emphasized that the wife need not follow her husband if he were to go against "right reason" or "her dignity as a wife"—no small exceptions—but nevertheless, Pius XI ended with, "For if the man is the head, the woman is the heart, and as he occupies the chief place in ruling, so she may and ought to claim for herself the chief place in love" (no. 27).

Pope Pius XII (1939–1958) also clearly held this view of the marital relationship and spoke of it frequently, although it did not find a prominent place in his encyclicals. When Pope John XXIII (1958–1963) mentioned marital roles, he also used this traditional language.

We then come to the documents of Vatican II. The purpose of Vatican II was, according to Pope John XXIII, an attempt at *aggiornamento*: a renewal and an updating. Its goal was to respond to the signs of the times and to speak clearly and convincingly to the modern world. Marriage is addressed most prominently in the

1965 document *The Church in the Modern World* (*Gaudium et Spes*). Despite a lengthy section on marriage, it does not repeat the traditional statements regarding headship. The closest the document comes to addressing marital roles is when it calls for "an affectionate sharing of souls between the married couple and their commitment to cooperation in the children's upbringing" (no. 52). *Gaudium et Spes* is well known by canon lawyers and other leaders in the Church as the document that introduced, more wholeheartedly, the importance in marriage of the mutual self-gift of the married couple. Karol Wojtyla, who contributed to the text, was to champion the same concept years later as Pope John Paul II.

After the council, Pope Paul VI (1963–1978) spoke out forcefully on the need to offer women justice in the workplace and in the social sphere, but he did not speak clearly either for or against the concept of headship in marriage.

The Teachings of Pope John Paul II
The task remained for our current pope, Pope John Paul II (1978–present), to take the next step. Pope John Paul II sees himself as a champion of human love, especially of the love between a woman and a man in marriage. He has devoted an extraordinary amount of time, energy, and attention to this topic—possibly more than any other pope in history. His 1981 apostolic exhortation *On the Family* (*Familiaris Consortio*) dwelled on marriage in the context of family life in general. He also focused on this topic in his weekly audiences between September 1979 and November 1984. These presentations were later collected by editor John Grabowski in a volume entitled *The Theology of the Body: Human Love in the Divine Plan.*[1]

Pope John Paul II also repeated and sharpened his reflections on marriage in his 1988 letter *On the Dignity and Vocation of Women* (*Mulieris Dignitatem*). In these writings he clearly moved away from the concept of headship, often quoting Ephesians 5:22: "Wives should be subordinate to their husbands as to the Lord. For the husband is head of his wife just as Christ is head of the church, he himself the savior of the body. As the church is subordinate to Christ, so wives should be subordinate to their husbands in everything." Pope John Paul II, in previous writings, had gone over this passage in painstaking detail: "The husband and the wife are in fact 'subject to one another,' and are mutually subordinated to one another. . . . Love makes the husband simultaneously subject to the wife and thereby subject to the Lord himself, just as the wife to the husband" (*The Theology of the Body*, 310). A few years later, referring to the same passage, the pope repeated and emphasized this point in *Mulieris Dignitatem*:

> The author knows that this way of speaking, so profoundly rooted in the customs and religious tradition of the time, is to be understood and carried out in a new way: as a *"mutual subjection out of reverence for Christ"* (cf. Eph 5:21). This is especially true because the husband is called the "head" of the wife as Christ is the head of the Church; he is so in order to give "himself up for her" (Eph 5:25), and giving himself up for her means giving up even his own life. However, whereas in the relationship between Christ and the Church the subjection is only on the part of the Church, in the relationship between husband and wife the "subjection" is not one-sided but mutual. (no. 24)

Clearly, this is a new development in the teaching regarding the relation of man and woman in marriage. How does the pope justify it? He calls this understanding of the mutual subjection in marriage the "gospel innovation," contrasting it with the Genesis presentation where Eve is told, "Your urge shall be for your husband, and he shall be your master" (Gn 3:16). For the pope, his statements are the latest step in the long process of the emancipation of women from the effects of sin; he calls it the "evil inheritance" begun in the garden but freed by Jesus Christ. In speaking about this history, the pope is unequivocal:

> The "innovation" of Christ is a fact: it constitutes the unambiguous content of the evangelical message and is the result of the Redemption. However, the awareness that in marriage there is mutual "subjection of the spouses out of reverence for Christ," and not just that of the wife to the husband, must gradually establish itself in hearts, consciences, behaviour and customs. This is a call which from that time onwards, does not cease to challenge succeeding generations; it is a call which people have to accept ever anew. (*Mulieris Dignitatem*, no. 24)

The pope then suggests a parallel between the gradual release of Christian tradition from the condoning of slavery and the gradual emancipation of women. What does he mean by comparing the subordination of women and slavery?

The pope is not saying that headship is slavery. He is saying that Paul urged masters to be good to their slaves, and slaves to obey their masters, without—in Scripture—saying slavery was wrong. However, over a considerable length of time, it became clear that the overall message of the Gospel was to condemn slavery. In the same way, although Paul urged headship and submission to the couples of his time, Pope John Paul II is saying that the overall message and thrust of the Gospels is calling men and women to a new kind of equal partnership. Indeed, the pope references other places in Scripture where specific injunctions against women are recorded. These include women being veiled in church, women not speaking at public services, and women only asking questions of their husbands in private. Few in the Church are suggesting that we return to following those rules—even though they are clearly stated in Scripture.

Complementarity

Is the pope saying that men and women are the same and have no differences or distinctive characteristics? Not at all. His appreciation for the special characteristics and distinctive gifts of men and women—which he calls "complementarity"—is obvious in a hundred different places. Perhaps it could best be described like this. On one side of orthodox teaching would be the erroneous belief that men and women, beyond the obvious differences in anatomy, are absolutely the same. This "unisex" approach does not square up with church teaching. Too far to the other side, however, would be the teaching that God has ordained that the man, because he is a man, has been granted in marriage a unilateral leadership role. As I understand the pope, his position is that men and women have both gifts in common and gifts distinctive of their sex, all of which they are called to offer to each other in a marriage partnership of equal authority.

It might be worthwhile to look at other authoritative documents whose purpose is to guide the life and teachings of the Church. The 1983 *Code of Canon Law*, which by its nature deals with rights and obligations within the Church, says much about the marriage relationship; however, it does not speak of headship. The closest canon relating to the subject is c. 1135, "The Mutual Obligations of the Spouses": "Each spouse has an equal duty and right to those things which belong to the partnership of conjugal life."

Perhaps even more telling for our purposes is the *Catechism of the Catholic Church*, which was officially promulgated in 1994. The *Catechism* was developed expressly to offer a sound source for those responsible for teaching the faith to others. Certainly the *Catechism* devotes considerable attention to marriage, both in its treatment of the sacraments and in its treatment of the Ten Commandments. A theology of marriage is presented in some detail, including considerable attention to the distinctiveness of the sexes: using the pope's word, "complementarity." Yet within all of this attention, there is no mention of headship. The closest the *Catechism* comes to this area is when it quotes the aforementioned statement in *Gaudium et Spes*: "The family is a *privileged community* called to achieve a 'sharing of thought and common deliberation by the spouses as well as their eager cooperation as parents in the children's upbringing'" (no. 2206).

Men's Ministry Today

So what should we teach at our men's conferences and at our Catholic Bible study groups, in our pamphlets and in our books? Some would say that 1,960 years of teaching on headship (i.e., from Christ's birth until Vatican II) wins out over the teaching of the last forty years on mutual subjection and partnership. If we follow that line of reasoning, though, we encounter other problems. The task of the pope is not simply to put his words alongside the words of earlier popes but to offer us the teaching of the Church for this time, at this place. His task is to synthesize and further explain what has come before and to offer us what the word of God is today.

The phrase "development of doctrine," which has been associated with Cardinal John Henry Newman, means that the Church is always searching to express the truth of God's revelation more accurately, more fully, and more completely, in every generation. It is clear that the doctrine relating to women and their position vis-à-vis men has developed over the centuries. We have only to look back at such giants in the faith as St. Augustine and St. Thomas Aquinas, who are arguably the two most influential theologians in the history of the Church. They were progressives in their day regarding women, yet they both clearly considered women to be defective or incomplete creatures compared to men. Yet they advanced the doctrine beyond where it had been before them. Something similar might be said of various other theologians and popes since then. Pope John Paul II obviously sees himself as continuing in that long line of development. Those who would accuse the pope of "selling out" on headship must confront the fact that he has shown no fear in maintaining other very unpopular and politically incorrect doctrines, which he might have jettisoned if jettisoning was on his mind.

In light of Pope John Paul II's clear and constant teaching for twenty-five years and the lack of support for headship in either the *Code of Canon Law* or the *Catechism of the Catholic Church*, I do not believe we are justified in teaching that headship is the model for marriage in the Catholic Church. Indeed, to be in union with the Holy Father in this area, we would need to teach that men and women have gifts in common and gifts more distinctive to their gender, but that these gifts are called to be shared in marriage in a relationship of equal authority.

How might this affect men and women who have modeled their marriage along headship lines? Perhaps not as much as one might think. As I mentioned at the beginning of this article, many writers have brought nuances to the concept of headship, including the introduction of concepts such as "servant leadership" and "sacrificial love." Clearly, the emphasis is not on the man's getting his own way, but on his making decisions that put his wife and family first. There is also an insistence on careful listening and attention to all before any decisions are made. Whenever possible, one strives for a true meeting of the minds and hearts before any action is taken.

The more completely and unselfishly a man commits to this more nuanced understanding of headship, the closer he comes to mutuality. Indeed, I get the impression in some cases that only the word "headship" remains, while the actual experience is one of mutuality. It only remains to re-frame the call, from one of headship to one of partnership. The call is to a new concept of leadership, where leadership does not adhere only to the man but is rather a gift of the spirit to the man and to the woman. The Apostle Paul also said, "Defer to one another out of reverence for Christ," and in these words we can also hear Pope John Paul II's call to mutual self-donation, a call that requires, from each partner, both surrender and initiative. ■

Dr. James Healy *is the Director of the Center for Family Ministry of the Diocese of Joliet, Illinois. He was the founding President of Illinois Catholic Family Ministries and has served as an adviser to the United States Conference of Catholic Bishops' Committee on Marriage and Family Life.*

SUGGESTED FURTHER READING FROM THE VATICAN AND BISHOPS' CONFERENCE

Vatican: *Familiaris Consortio (On the Family)*; *Letter to Families from Pope John Paul II*; *Mulieris Dignitatem (On the Dignity and Vocation of Women)*; *The Theology of the Body* (Daughters of St. Paul); *The Truth and Meaning of Human Sexuality: Guidelines for Education Within the Family*

U.S. Catholic Bishops: *The Call to Family, Community, and Participation*; *Faithful to Each Other Forever*; *Families: Black and Catholic, Catholic and Black*; *Family Guide for Using Media*; *A Family Perspective in Church and Society*; *Follow the Way of Love: A Pastoral Message of the U.S. Catholic Bishops to Families*; *Human Sexuality: A Catholic Perspective for Education and Lifelong Learning*; *To Last a Lifetime* (video); *Your Family and Cyberspace*

See p. 92 for ordering information.

NOTE

1. John Paul II, *The Theology of the Body: Human Love in the Divine Plan*, ed. John Grabowski (St. Paul, Minn.: Daughters of St. Paul, 1997).

Catholic Men as Disciples in the Workplace

BY JAMES L. NOLAN

When we speak of the workplace, we are talking generally about the place where we are "doing"—thus we seek spirituality *for doers*. To find out what is really going on in the busyness of our "doing," we must reflect theologically on our personal experiences. My personal experiences have been shaped by a model of theological reflection, which is at the core of the men's group, prayer group, and Woodstock Business Conference described below. I invite each of you to reflect theologically on your own experiences to see if you might find this model helpful as you examine and refine your work for the men of the Church.

A theological reflection process should include these steps:
- What, why, when, who, and how? Describe the experience, making sure you include appropriate details.
- Use your intelligence and reason to name what is really going on, or go back and get the missing data.
- Judge what is good and worthwhile in the experience under examination.
- What are you going to do about it? Choose to enhance the good and diminish the negative aspects of the experience.

It seems strange to think of oneself as a disciple in the workplace, and men often speak of a gap between their faith experiences and their lives at work. They conclude that the claim that God loves us looks terribly naive in the face of the harsh reality of work. Yet today men are seeking new ways, more effective channels for encouragement, and fresh instrumentalities to bring their religious faith to the whole of their lives in mature and responsible ways. I want to highlight three initiatives that have promoted effective and authentic integration of faith, family, and work and have empowered men to become disciples in the workplace.

Men's Groups

About fifteen years ago a couple dozen men gathered at a family weekend retreat sponsored by the parish. One of the men, a psychiatrist, posted a notice that read, "Men's Group Meeting—after lunch." No one knew what to expect. This had never happened before in this parish. The person who posted the note began by noting that he had no idea what to expect—but since women had been gathering for conversation for years, why not give it a try? At the start of the meeting, he asked a series of questions:

- How many of you had a best buddy—someone you shared everything with, secrets and all—when you were a boy? (All hands went up.)
- What about when you were a teenager? (Most hands went up.)
- How many of your wives have a best friend—another woman whom she confides in? (Again, most hands went up.)
- How many of you now have a best buddy or friend, other than your wife, whom you can talk things over with—about what is happening at work, the family, your faith, things that really matter? (No hands went up.)

Then he said, "Now that might be a clue why the women are outliving us."

After exploring the implications of this informal survey in terms of friendships, health, and quality of life, the men in the group promised to learn each other's names and meet once a month for the next six months to see what would happen.

They kept their promise and began monthly meetings. Soon, it was clear that once a month was too infrequent; they decided to meet every two weeks. The ground rules that they developed are quite simple. Almost every other Saturday, someone offers his home for the early morning meeting. It begins at 7:30 A.M. and ends at 9:00. Another volunteers to bring bagels and donuts, and a third brings juice. Coffee is the responsibility of the meeting's host. Three or four times a year a mailing goes out—or the information is posted on the Internet—with the dates, locations, and assignments for the next several months. Fortunately, a sheaf of maps accompanies each mailing.

As time went on, new men joined the group at the invitation of a friend and stayed. The mailing list—which eventually became an e-mail list—now has more than one hundred entries. Some men have left the area but reconnect with the group when back in town. Others find themselves unable to make meetings for some time but express amazement upon their return that they can find themselves right back at home again.

There is no fixed agenda, no officers, no dues. Meetings begin generally with each person's stating his name, and then discussion takes off almost spontaneously. What the group has done over time is build friendships and community within a context of *shared spiritual values*. The discussions involve personal sharing about life's milestones and day-to-day challenges. Prayer lives, faith concerns, and matters relating to children and parents, work and jobs, and even larger societal issues are often grist for the mill. The quality of listening is profound. Men support each other as they try to live Christian values in family, in personal relationships, and in the larger community. Meetings have seen expressions of the deepest wisdom, most poignant stories, and hearty laughter. My children told me that they knew it was men's group when they woke up to loud, full-bodied laughter early on a Saturday morning.

The men's group meetings produced some visible offshoots such as weekend retreats, Christmas parties, numerous social justice projects, and the most important product: friendships—sometimes life-saving ones—that have formed and deepened over the years.

One important conversation was about the relationship a man has—or had—with his father. In the men's group, a substantial majority said that their relationship with their father had not been good. Some men shared what had been done to reconcile: spend time, forgive, ask forgiveness, ask your father to enter into a closer relationship with his family, ask the questions that needed to be asked. Men also told of the steps they had taken to address past hurts and find mutual common ground. In the men's group old wounds healed.

Prayer Group

A little over sixteen years ago, our pastor inaugurated a number of Scripture-based prayer groups hosted in people's homes. Typically, these groups gathered on a weekly basis during Advent and Lent to reflect on the Sunday Gospel. Like the men's groups, the format was simple: the group gathers briefly for social time; participants are called to prayer with a short reading, music, or silence; participants read the Sunday Gospel and respond, reflecting on what they heard or felt. Often the group recounts the points made—or that should have been made—in homilies heard the Sunday before. After the discussion, the Gospel is read a second time, and people pray over it. The meeting concludes with the Lord's Prayer.

These Scripture-based prayer groups continued to form in our parish each Advent and Lent. Some have been in continuous operation, meeting biweekly during the "off-seasons," for more than fifteen years, with fresh faces joining every season. Participants give testimony to the power of the prayer groups as they witness to the parish community before each new sign-up season. They recount how participation has been for them life-giving, faith-deepening. New insights result when the richness of the Gospel is shared with such seriousness and groundedness. They say it has inspired their lives. Community and friendships are formed. Support is available in times of need and sorrow, as it is in times of happiness and joy. Shared opportunities for spiritual growth are explored. Friends hold themselves to account.

Other than the logistics of finding people to open their homes for the meetings and helping new participants find their groups, no official leadership, agenda, or cost is needed for prayer groups. The aim of deepened spirituality is realized by openness to the Spirit grounded in prayerful reflection on the word of God.

Woodstock Business Conference

For eight years, I have served as executive director of the Woodstock Business Conference, a network of business leaders and professionals established to develop a corporate culture consistent with Judeo-Christian tradition. These individuals (mostly men) formed more than eighteen chapters in America and Canada to integrate their faith, family, and professional lives and to exercise a beneficial influence upon society at large. The conference, which is grounded in the Roman Catholic tradition, welcomes believers who are open to and respectful of one another's religious traditions. It is committed to the conviction that ethics and values grow out of one's religious heritage.

Participants offer each other a kind of peer ministry in support of this mission. Over the years, a meeting process developed that has been credited with the success the conference has enjoyed. Real issues arising from the concrete experiences of members are surfaced and addressed in a manner that produces small steps, incremental changes. Over time, we have seen positive results and significant growth in the participants.

This process takes place in monthly chapter meetings running about an hour and a half. The meetings are held at the same time and place each month and begin and end on time so that busy people can count on and set aside the time on their calendars. The meeting format includes certain elements:
- Self-introductions
- An opening prayer
- Reading of the mission statement
- Scripture reading followed by a period of silence and then a sharing of insights on the passage
- Discussion of the topic for the meeting
- Reflection and evaluation of the meeting
- Closing prayer

Let me tell you about one situation that focused on the question of loyalty. The meeting began with the biblical account of Judas's fatal miscalculation. We reflected on the passage in which Judas, wracked with guilt, takes the thirty pieces of silver he gained for betraying Jesus and tries to return the blood money to his new "friends," the high priests. Of course they tell Judas to get lost. "Look at how Judas found himself out of favor with what he thought was his new team," observed one business manager. Another confessed, "This is the first time I ever felt sorry for Judas. Here he left Jesus' inner circle to take up with the establishment. He thought he was going to be accepted because he delivered Jesus to them as promised. But his so-called new friends just turned their backs on him."

Before the meeting, they read a *Wall Street Journal* article about investment advisors who received huge signing bonuses to switch from their old firms to new ones, bringing their customers with them. Several talked about how they had been "bitten" by bright young professionals whom they trained and mentored, only to see them "jump ship" and go to work for competitors. "There is just no loyalty these days," said one participant. Some men even told how they gave the company all they had for twenty years or more (in some cases losing marriages and families along the way), and then found themselves out on the street after their firms were acquired. One executive confessed to what sounded like a lapse of loyalty. He was running the star division of an industrial machinery company, bringing his people along, getting them "invested" in the work. He promised them a great future as members of his team. One day a headhunter called him and offered him a lucrative opportunity with a competing organization. He took it! "I had to consider my family even if it wasn't altogether fair to the team."

About a month later, another executive in the company told the gathering that given the bleak financial assessments, he and his top management felt they had to close the group's division. This executive, remembering conversations about loyalty, felt he had to break the news personally to the employees. Most CEOs would have sent a memo on Friday afternoon or assigned their human resources manager to the task. But this man said, "I had to look my people in the eye." Moreover, he was determined to carry out the closings in the most humane way possible. He made sure the employees were given extended medical benefits and hired an outplacement firm to help them find new jobs. Where possible, he absorbed the laid-off people elsewhere within the organization. Those who heard this story affirmed that they too had grown morally and ethically. They said that they could better see the good and evil in their work lives and elsewhere. They sensed that they are empowered to choose and act more responsibly, and their chapter meetings became "monthly moral checkups." They reported that they became "better spiritual leaders back at work," and they found the necessary encouragement to take innovative and effective action and to initiate needed change.

A Three-Point Plan: Engagement, Community, and Prayer

What do these examples suggest for us in terms of fostering discipleship? I see three essentials: engagement, community, and prayer. These elements form the backbone for a vital three-point plan for discipleship.

1. *Engagement*

The first essential is *engagement*, which describes an attitude and commitment, as well as the day-to-day activities of a calling or profession. The good we can do at work and at home for our family, individuals, and society is far too important to ignore. We are all called to collaborate in God's creative and redemptive work, called to use our skills and talents for the greater good. Human activity lies properly within the framework of the collaboration with God to which every human being is called. Today we are called to echo this divine design and collaborate with our Creator in the transformation of the world according to his plan.

The notion of our collaboration with God conveys the idea that human work is a sharing in the divine work of creation. Pope John Paul II has stressed this idea in his writings time and time again. By our proper use of the wealth of spiritual and material resources given to us by the Creator, we are called to contribute to the progress of society.

The obvious implication of the call to collaborate is not to run away or withdraw from society; nor should we hide our heads in the sand, constructing compartments to wall off concerns generated by our religious sensibilities. Compartmentalization is quite popular today. Seeing one's life as a kind of vocation or calling is one way to assume the attitude, disposition, and commitment necessary to answer the call to collaborate with God in his work. The task at hand is to bring one's whole self (mind, heart, and soul) to each day's challenges and opportunities wherever they might be found. Each of the three examples above, in very simple ways, reinforces the call to engagement. They validate that what goes on at work counts. They provide safe places for discussion and understanding. They facilitate friendships and mutual support.

2. *Community*

The second essential ingredient is *community*. In our very secular culture, being a person who affirms that his religious faith informs his life can be very lonely. Persons seeking integration and the strengthening of relationships with God, others, and the world want something more than skill at bracketing off or suppressing religious concerns. This requires a community of support and encouragement. Our Catholic faith community—going back in time, embedded in the present, and facing the future—can help to channel and encourage our desire to do what is right, to be good disciples.

Evil and sin exist in the world. We all sin and fall short of our goals. Systems and structures are present in our society that promote evil, as well as support goodness and justice. Alone, we might easily overlook the absurdity of evil and sin. Alone, we might lack the power to confront the structures or systems at work that encourage evil. But within a faith community, we are spurred to recognize what we would otherwise overlook and to question what would otherwise remain buried in ignorance or prejudice.

As a member of the men's group described above, I recently wrote an e-mail to all the members:

> As I reflect over the events of this busy day, I realize again (as I have many times before) how important our men's group is to me and to many others. I knew I was missing being a part of the group, but not until I came back to this morning's meeting after being absent for several months did I realize just how much I missed the group. Thank you for being there! It was really great to see everyone and to share our thoughts and prayers—as we so easily do with each other.

In *Bowling Alone,* Robert Putnam identified individualism and loneliness as the hallmarks of our contemporary life. He and other authors cite causes such as the following:

- Working longer hours
- Commuting for long periods of time
- Spending more time as working parents outside the home in child raising, carpooling, and helping with homework
- Watching more television, "the entertainment box that keeps America cocooned at home instead of at community meetings"[1]

As one men's group member noted, they are busy on Saturdays but choose to attend these early morning sessions because they find support and encouragement with others. In collaboration, we foster the habits and practices that promote discipleship.

3. *Prayer*

The third necessary ingredient in discipleship is *prayer.* We are not alone. In fact, we are loved by God into being and empowered in life by God's grace. As Catholics we respond at Eucharist. We give thanks. By prayer we keep our communication lines with God open and supple. The benefits of small faith-sharing groups, spiritual direction, and the charisms of our religious orders point the ways to fuller, more fruitful prayer opportunities. While no particular form or method of prayer can be said to be tailored specifically for a busy businessman or professional, those with a verbal bent find praying with the Psalms a particularly compatible communication pathway.

We also need to probe our own religious faith to know God, God's works, and God's will for us. Such study can itself be a very positive form of prayer. The same diligence and energy spent in learning what is necessary for our jobs, markets, products, and services can—when focused on the history, practices, and grounding of our religious faith—produce rare and enriching fruit.

Finding God at Work

Recent events have heightened the desire to focus on what really counts, to return to what is essential and basic in our lives. After September 11, my conversations with members of the men's group, the prayer group, and the local Woodstock Business Conference chapter underscore this fact. Our world right now seems to be in the middle of a profound sea change affecting all aspects of life: social, cultural, economic, and political. A shorthand term for this is globalization. Business, economic exchange, commercial transactions, exploding technologies, and challenges to "ways of life" are driving our lives. The whole world is the arena where the changes are being played out.

At the same time we are seeing another phenomenon in America. People now, more than ever, want to integrate their whole selves, integrate who they are with what they do. Some have named this the *spirituality and work movement*. Observers like Laura Nash at Harvard Business School talk about an "explosion of spirituality in the workplace." People are coming to recognize the deep-seated drive within each one of us to use our talents, intelligence, and imagination for the greater good. The changes we call "globalization" and "spirituality in the workplace" are not unrelated.

When I speak about spirituality in the workplace with business, professional, and political groups, people doubt that it is even possible in a time of rapid change, shifting boundaries, faint allegiances, and globalization to lead a spiritual life in the world of work. They talk about a decline in loyalty and positive relationships between organizations and individuals and between workers and their organizations. It seems that everyone is a free agent now. We see diminished professionalism in the practice of law and medicine. Individualism and selfishness seemed to be elevated and rewarded, defeating teamwork and community.

How might we lead a spiritual life at work in the middle of all this mess? Our faith tells us that this can be done—by finding God at work. At first blush this may seem to be an outrageous thought. What saint spent a workday behind a computer screen? How many famous holy men or women have we heard of who taught middle-school kids, worked in the ER, prepared tax returns, or served as the CEO of a multinational Fortune 500 company? Not many.

But that is not the point. The point is to understand what we are really doing when we work. As an exercise to help understand what we are doing, I ask the people to take a simple test that works with any group or calling:

- List five satisfying, exciting, wonderful things you can say about your work. Review the list and reflect on what it says about your work.
- Then list five things you find most troubling or discouraging about your work. Reflect on this list and what it says about your work and your own quest for integration.
- What are you going to do about it?

After considering their responses to the first question above, people begin to understand that what they are doing is good and are moved to gratitude. This is particularly true in a session that begins with Scripture reflection, as the Woodstock Business Conference meetings do. Upon considering the next questions in the simple test above, the participants think about how the negatives they listed might be improved. Above all, they recognize that there are elements of both progress and decline in what we do at work. By beginning with what is positive and being moved to gratitude, people are open to seeing God at work, laboring in our world. We can be more open to speaking about partnering with God whose law is written on our hearts. We see his work being accomplished in history, working its way over time. And we see that we are right in the middle of all this. We are God's creations, called to be co-workers in his project. We are invited to use our intelligence, energy, savvy, and all that we care about to that end. When we understand and choose the positive and recognize and diminish the negative, when we work and make life better in any way, we are not alone. We are in league with God, being led by the Holy Spirit. We are disciples.

Our work, whether at home or on the job, is much more than a job category or a pay grade. It is where we realize who we are. This is where we spend so much of our day, where we know, choose, and do what is best. This is the place where we can truly team up with God—God, who is already there, working in us, moving us to work for the greater good.

How do we know this? Members of the groups described above have learned to check the evidence within. We see the dynamic at work that drives us to seek what is true when we ask who, what, when, where, and how. We feel the dynamic that pushes us to choose what is valuable and worthwhile. We want to know the truth and to do what is right. You do not have to be a believer to be asking these questions and making these judgments. We are doing it all the time. It is part of being alive. Because we are believers, we acknowledge that it is the hand of God leading us, the love of God poured into our hearts by the Holy Spirit.

In each of these groups and from all sides, we see the desire for completeness and wholeness, the drive to integrate all of who we are, particularly who and what we are at work. We want to find God at work. Contemporary spiritual writers like Ronald Rolheiser and Michael Downey call this drive and desire the stepping-stone to spirituality.

Long ago the prophet Micah berated the leaders of Israel for ripping the people off. The leaders charged huge sums for lavish sacrifices and led corrupt lives, modeling the greediest behavior. Micah predicted horrible consequences for them. He reminded his listeners that even the most extravagant of offerings to God would not alter the judgments they had merited. Then, he offered his famous advice, a game plan for spiritual success: "You have been told, oh man, what is good, and what the Lord requires of you: only to do the right and to love goodness, and to walk humbly with your God" (Mi 6:8).

Conclusion

Catholic men are called today to be disciples. The events of September 11 served to sharpen that focus. Whatever our jobs or state of life might be, we carry the challenge to bring peace, justice, and joy to the world. One who is aware of his desire for integration and in touch with the inner drive for the transcendent is called to a spiritual way of being—to engage and live the same values and behaviors in the office, clinic, classroom, or courthouse as in the home and at church. The groups I mentioned and their simple ways of proceeding foster this awareness and burnish this desire.

Our religious faith challenges our notions and behaviors by promoting prayerful reflection and disciplined lives. A religious horizon empowers us to recognize important questions as our actions affect the lives of those we encounter and the structures and systems at work. We must engage this horizon using our intelligence, ability to reason, ability to make and carry out responsible choices, and ability to love. Alone, it is hard do this well. Community sustains us in a time of change. We are supported by healthy relationships with our families, neighbors, coworkers, and faith communities. We are empowered to be disciples when we pray and when we "do the right, love goodness, and walk humbly with our God." ∎

Mr. James L. Nolan *is Vice President for Institutional Advancement at the Washington Theological Union. He formally served as Executive Director of the Woodstock Business Conference. Mr. Nolan lectures and writes on topics including professions and spirituality, the integration of faith and work, and business and professional ethics.*

SUGGESTED FURTHER READING FROM THE VATICAN AND BISHOPS' CONFERENCE

Vatican: *Laborem Exercens (On Human Work)*

U.S. Catholic Bishops: *And God Said It Was Good: Catholic Theology and the Environment; Being Neighbor: The Catechism and Social Justice; Bring Down the Walls* (video); *Economic Justice for All; Everyday Christianity: To Hunger and Thirst for Justice; Faithful Citizenship; The Harvest of Justice Is Sown in Peace; In All Things Charity; Principles, Prophecy, and a Pastoral Response; Stewardship: A Disciple's Response*

See p. 92 for ordering information.

NOTE

1. Robert Putnam, *Bowling Alone: The Collapse and Revival of American Community* (New York: Simon & Schuster, 2000).

Fathers, Sons, and Brothers: Catholic Men Transforming the World

BY BISHOP MICHAEL W. WARFEL

There once was a man who searched for meaning in his life, and he happened upon a group of people being baptized in a river. Touched by their singing and the joy on their faces, he went down to the river and got in line to be baptized. When it was his turn, the minister grabbed him and immersed him in the water. As he came up, coughing and gasping for air, he heard the baptizer ask, "Did you find the Lord?" He quickly responded, "No!" Hearing his negative response, the baptizer plunged him once again under the water. As he allowed him back up to the surface, the baptizer asked again, "Did you find the Lord?" "No!" responded the man. This continued again and again. On the ninth time that the man surfaced, hearing the persistent baptizer ask, "Did you find the Lord?" he responded, "No! But wait a minute! Are you sure this is where he went under?"

The Eucharistic Life

The foundational dynamic of our faith is baptism in Christ. That, at least, is the claim of our faith. It is a celebration of new life in the risen Lord. Of course, when I speak of baptismal life as such, I mean more than merely being washed in a water bath during a religious ceremony at some time during our lives. I mean a sacramental ritual that expresses a faith-filled relationship in Christ, that we have died to sin and have arisen transformed. Baptism is not solely about our initiation into a system or into an organization we call the Church. It is that, but more deeply: it celebrates a relationship meant *to be* (or at least *to become*, in the case of an infant or a child) one that is intimate and personal. People who are baptized into Christ are expected to know more than just information about Jesus, his life, and what he taught. Those who desire to follow Christ and embrace his Gospel not only know *about* Jesus but they *know* Jesus. They have discovered the Lord of life!

Christian life flows primarily from a relationship with God in Christ. It is much more than knowledge about the faith. The doctrines of the Church, while vitally important for living Christian faith well, do not have a practical impact in the life of an individual until they are grounded in a relationship with Christ. It is when people have such a relationship that they have the strength and the courage, the desire and the faith, to embody the teachings of Christian faith in their day-to-day living and to value them as a light to guide their way through life.

Without a strong relationship with the Lord, people do not have the endurance, the vigor, nor the desire to embrace the Gospel of Christ everywhere and at all times. Nor do they value necessarily the whole of his Gospel and the teachings of his Church. Do you recall the Parable of the Sower in Mark's Gospel? Only the seed that fell on good soil yielded a crop that sprang up, increased, and produced fruit of thirty-, sixty-, and a hundredfold. I believe that the manner of lifestyle that best reflects this is called "Eucharistic." Individuals who have a faith that is based in a real relationship with the Lord are individuals who become Eucharistic. By appreciating the gift of life and salvation that they have received in Christ, they want to lead a life that bears fruit for the Kingdom of God. I think Catholics ought deeply to appreciate this given the importance we place on sacramental worship. Eucharist truly is the summit toward which the Church's activities are directed and the font from which the Church's ministry flows.

Those who most model fully Eucharistic life in Christ are the saints. A parish next to my cathedral in Juneau, Alaska, has a wide stairwell climbing up to a second-floor hall. On the wall alongside the stairwell hang about thirty photos or drawings of holy women and men with brief narratives describing why they are considered holy. Some are canonized, such as Sts. Francis, Claire of Assisi, Katherine Drexel, Josephine Bakita, and Thomas More. Others, while not canonized, are recognized as having manifested a high degree of holiness in their lives and as having witnessed to the Gospel in some profound way, such as Dorothy Day, Fr. Miguel Pro, Franz Jaggerstater, Mother Teresa, and Archbishop Oscar Romero. The activity of their lives has caused so many to recognize holiness in these men and women. They were able to grasp what so many Christians fail to grasp, that is, what it means to be Eucharistic. They understood the essential connection between the Body of Christ they worship "on the altar" and the Body of Christ who stood with them "before the altar." Not only did their spiritualities cause them to focus on Christ in their prayer and worship; it led them to so enflesh his life that their lives were translated into Eucharistic service. They recognized Christ in their brothers and sisters—especially their sisters and brothers most physically and spiritually in need. Such holy people showed how much they loved God by how concretely they loved God's people.

Frail little Mother Teresa began her day for years with adoration before the Blessed Sacrament and Mass. What she is known for, however, is her utter commitment to serving the world's poor and the most defenseless of persons. What she did was to make the essential connection!

Dorothy Day, via a different path, likewise was led to a pattern of daily prayer and Eucharist. What she is known for, however, is her unqualified commitment to the needy homeless of New York City and her work to change the social structures that lead to poverty. She made the essential connection!

St. John Chrysostom, preaching in the latter part of the fourth century, verbalized so well what they lived:

> Do you want to honor Christ's body? Then do not scorn him in his nakedness, nor honor him here in the church with silken garments while neglecting him outside where he is cold and naked. For he who said: This is my body, and made it so with his words, also said: You saw me hungry and did not feed me, and inasmuch as you did not do it for one of these, the least of my brothers, you did not do it for me. What we do here in the church requires a pure heart, not special garments; what we do outside requires great dedication.

Such holiness can and ought to be sought by each of us—any man who claims to be a follower of Christ. Obviously it must be done within our own time and place in history and with the particular gifts with which God has blessed us. What is required is to respond to the grace of God available to us always and everywhere through the Spirit of Jesus. Take for example, the patron saint of missions, St. Thérèse of Lisieux. She did nothing especially extraordinary in her life. But what she did do was to seek holiness within the humble and ordinary circumstances of her convent and did so with great fidelity, practicing her "little way." The "secret" of her holiness was living her faith in an extraordinary way. She responded to the grace of God within the circumstances of her time and place in history as best and as fully as she could. Is not this what each of us is to do with our own lives?

Some years ago, I was in Guayaquil, Ecuador, traveling with a priest who had a friend he wanted to visit. We stopped at the hospital where the friend worked. She was a nurse in a leper ward. Once I overcame my hesitancy, and after I had been assured that I was not going to contract leprosy, I entered the ward. I was able to observe the staff at work and their interactions with the patients, about fifty in number. We located the nurse friend in the room of a man who had been eaten up by the disease. What I encountered, surprisingly, was not sadness or anger or despair, but joy and peace. The nurse was a faith-filled person who not only took care of the man's health, but made it known that she deeply cared for the man. While we were in the room, the man kept expressing his thankfulness for having someone in his life who truly cared for him. I was touched by the interaction of love and caring between them. Not only was she a Christ to her patient, he was a Christ to his nurse. In their interaction I saw God.

All of these examples provide an illustration of the essential connection. Having received the gift of life and salvation from God in Christ, there is a corresponding obligation to share the gift of this life with others. When we do this, we are Eucharistic.

Following in the Footsteps of Jesus

The Gospel of Luke and the Acts of the Apostles (actually the second part of Luke's Gospel) establish a pattern for Christian life. Through them, the Evangelist describes an orderly account of the life of Christ and the spread of his Gospel "to the ends of the earth" by the earliest saints of the Church, that is, the holy men and women recalled on the pages of the New Testament. Of course we remember them, but not only to honor what they did. We remember them that we might know what we are supposed to do as Christians in our own day and age.

In the first part of Luke's Gospel, Jesus' nativity is narrated, then Luke continues with Jesus' public ministry and concludes with his passion and death, resurrection, and ascension to heaven. During his brief time on earth, Jesus calls forth a group of followers who then spread his Gospel and share their experience of his dying and rising throughout the world of their day. Nothing found in Luke's Gospel shows that this Gospel was taken anywhere much beyond the environs of Jerusalem. Rather, the Gospel proper is more concerned about following Jesus as a disciple and the invitation for the disciples to carry the cross each day after his example. As the disciples followed, they were led to Calvary and only then to the experience of the empty tomb and the resurrection of Jesus. The last scene from the Gospel is his ascension. Essentially, this is where Luke's Gospel stops.

Acts of the Apostles continues the story, beginning where the Gospel leaves off, at the ascension. Acts offers a portrait of the early Church as it developed and spread from Jerusalem to the center of the Roman Empire, the city of Rome itself. Filled with the Spirit of Jesus, his followers began to take his Gospel far and wide. They were apostles, believers sent to proclaim the Good News of salvation in Christ.

This pattern of being called and sent, depicted in the Gospel of Luke and the Acts of the Apostles, is for all believers of every time and place to embrace. In Christ, God calls us to follow in the footsteps of Jesus by appropriating his Gospel into our daily lives. In Christ, God empowers us through the Spirit to proclaim the Gospel to "the ends of the earth." In other words, we are called to be both disciples who are formed in faith by Christ's Gospel and apostles who are sent to announce the Good News of salvation in Christ.

As members of the Church, we need to refresh regularly our memories about who we are (or better yet, *whose* we are) and what we are to be about. Called and formed as disciples, we are sent to proclaim Christ. As we were reminded by Pope John Paul II in his apostolic letter *Novo Millennio Ineunte* (*The Church in the Third Millennium*), we must "put out into the deep for a catch." *Duc in Altum!* This is a reference to the call of the first disciples from Luke's Gospel (Lk 5:4).

Members of the Body of Christ
Each of us, each Christian, is like a word. Words have function and meaning. Each particular word is a part of speech. Some are verbs and nouns, while others are adverbs, adjectives, and prepositions. Similarly, words tend to have specific meanings. The word "house" refers to a dwelling in which people live. "White" might refer to the color of the house, while "my" might inform people that the "white house" belongs to me. To have full meaning and purpose, words are used together in order to compose sentences, then paragraphs, and finally a complete story. Individual Christians have meaning and purpose in and of themselves. However, it is together, as members of the Body of Christ, that our full meaning and purpose as Christian are expressed.

Each member of the Church has a very unique role in the mission of the Church to proclaim Christ. No other person shares the exact time and space in history or the specific circumstances in life as any one of us. No other person has the exact same talents or the exact same personality. No one person who ever has existed or who will exist in the future is exactly like any one of us. Each of us shares Christ in the unique way that only we can share him. As such, we must never discount nor diminish the unique role each of us plays in bringing Christ to another person. In a very real sense, God depends on us all to do our part.

Men's Roles in the Church

When I was asked to provide a title for this presentation, I submitted "Father, Sons, and Brothers: Catholic Men Transforming the World." The title expresses my expectation for men in the Church. The experience of numerous men taking ownership for their faith gives me much hope. Each man is often a combination of the three roles I mention. We either are a father, a son, or a brother. The three terms are relational words that speak to the roles men have in society. They also speak to the roles men need to fill within the context of faith. As fathers, we have a life-giving role within the Church. What we say and what we do ought to buoy up others in faith and bring life. As sons, we have a life-receiving role within the Church. We are not sufficient in ourselves to overcome all of life's problems and struggles; rather, we must be willing to be authored by the father of Jesus and allow his will to be ours. As brothers, we have a life-sharing role. We must remember that Christian faith, while personal, is never merely individual. It is through our interaction with others, as brothers in faith, that we best understand who we are as members of a Body of Christ.

It ought to be obvious that conversion and renewal must occur if we are to be effective witnesses of Christ. In fact, it seems that conversion experiences have led so many men to deeply commit to living their faith. In preparation for the symposium on men's ministries, I met with a group of diverse men with different experiences of growing up in the Church. All currently are quite involved in their parish communities, all are involved in some kind of ministry, and all are part of some kind of faith support group. The common denominator to their faith response was an experience of faith and sharing by other men. Through the sharing of faith with other men, they came to know Christ in a way they had not known earlier. In a real sense, Christ came alive for them and has made a significant difference in their lifestyles.

Christian Values and Conversion

Appropriation of Christian values involves regularly going against the current of the society in which we live. Too many destructive influences sway us from accomplishing our mission. Values of contemporary American culture—such as materialism, relativism, and individualism—can imperceptibly yet definitely sway us. To offset such influences calls for ongoing conversion of life and an enduring renewal of our discipleship. Like salmon that swim upstream against the current and only then are able to spawn and create new life, the Christian who values his or her faith must struggle against the influences that would lead to infidelity.

My presumption is that men are striving to grow in wisdom, age, and grace; are trying to walk faithfully in the way of the Lord; and are seeking to grow in their relationship with Christ. I realize well that we are at the same time affected to some degree by the influences of our day and age. The counter-Christian values found in culture and society often entice us to make choices contrary to the interests of our faith. If we are to remain faithful to Christ, we must commit to doing what is necessary for the relationship, not only to persevere, but to remain strong. Like tea that becomes strong only after the tea leaves have steeped in hot water for a sufficient period of time (otherwise the tea is nothing more than tinted and flavored water), we must be immersed into the life of the Risen Lord. What he taught, how he lived, the standards and principles he valued must be the measure for what we believe, the lifestyles we lead, and the values we hold. The more truly he is at the center of our lives (and at the center of all the members of the Church), the more fruitful and effective will be our witness, both individually as his disciples and collectively as a Church.

I believe that conversion always needs to be a part of our dialogue, both in the sense of an initial opening to Christ in a heartfelt way as well as the need of each person to surrender in a deeper way with each new day. Conversion to his Gospel is like a blind man who sees for the first time. It is also like a man who has his vision checked each year and discovers he needs to update his eyeglass prescription. Viewing life through the prism of faith produces in us a desire to share Christ. It helps us to appreciate not only why we must evangelize but also what we must do in order to evangelize. People who have been converted by the Gospel of Christ and know his power and presence in their lives will use their resources and energies to accomplish the Church's mission of proclaiming Christ

64

to the ends of the earth. In this light, the more Catholic men that can be brought to experience Christ deeply, the more effective will we be as church in our world.

I have a Chinese-born friend who grew up in Peru but has lived in the United States for quite some time. At one point in his life, he was not practicing his Catholic faith. Another man who worked at the same engineering firm as he did was a Baptist, and this man would invite regularly his coworkers to church. After a number of invitations, my friend told me that he actually decided to go with him one Sunday. He related that he had been warmly welcomed to the Baptist church and that the music and singing had been excellent while the preaching was challenging but inspiring. He said it truly had touched him. My friend said that as he reflected more on the experience, he decided that he needed to do something with his faith. He decided that what he should do, however, is not return to his coworker's church, but become active in his own Catholic Church. As he continued to reflect, he seemed to feel challenged by his Baptist friend in contrast to himself. The Baptist man told everyone about his faith, while no one knew that my friend was Catholic.

Evangelization

My guess is that the word "evangelization" is not used commonly among most Catholics. If it is, it is used to describe evangelical preachers. Rightly understood, however, it has a definite place in a typical Catholic's vocabulary and ought to be reclaimed. It comes from a Greek word that means "good news." As described in the U.S. bishops' pastoral plan for evangelization, *Go and Make Disciples*, it means "bringing the Good News of Jesus into every human situation and seeking to convert individuals and society by the divine power of the Gospel itself." To evangelize is to invite all people to conversion of mind and heart and to a Christ-centered way of life—in other words, a Eucharistic life.

Pope Paul VI wrote of evangelization in his 1968 apostolic letter *Evangelii Nuntiandi*. He noted that evangelization is the essential mission of the Church. Throughout the whole of his pontificate, Pope John Paul II has also spoken of the "New Evangelization" that needs to take place. This "New Evangelization" in no way means preaching a "new" Gospel; rather, it is a call to implement the Gospel anew: in new ways for a new millennium with a whole set of new ways of looking at life with a whole new set of problems.

In broad terms, I would like to suggest that evangelization has at least four major areas of interest. First, it is concerned with the active membership of the Church. This applies mainly to those who are Roman Catholic. Evangelization looks to their ongoing development and renewal, their nourishment, and their spiritual growth in Christ. In the context of this movement, we need to recall the significant number of Catholic men who are just "out there"; maybe Catholic, but inwardly searching for a means to live faith in more than just a peripheral way. The faith of the Church's membership must be nourished and nurtured. If not, it generally becomes stagnant and loses its vitality. As a muscle will atrophy if it is not exercised, so too will faith.

Second, evangelization needs to address the inactive members of the Catholic Church who for whatever reason feel alienated and disenfranchised. In the United States alone, there are roughly 17 million inactive Catholics. This makes them the second largest denomination in the country (behind active Catholics and ahead of Southern Baptists). It is the role of every Catholic person and community to provide welcome and understanding to those who find themselves outside the visible structures of the Church. Reaching out to these inactive Catholics—many of whom are hurting, wounded, angry, or frustrated—must be a normal part of the Church's activity.

Third, evangelization needs to speak to the unchurched millions who are not affiliated with any religious body, who have yet to demonstrate any response to God in their lives. Many of these unchurched individuals may in fact have a level of faith in their lives, but often it is imperfectly formed. Many others have yet to accept any kind of faith dimension in their lives, concentrating instead on secular pursuits. A vibrant Christian community provides the treasure of a life in Christ to those who search for meaning and purpose. The Catholic Church, in particular, offers a fullness of belief to those desiring to live a Christian faith.

Fourth, evangelization should foster ecumenical and interreligious relations in the spirit of Pope John Paul II's encyclical letter *Ut Unum Sint*. The prayer of Jesus was that all might be one. Somehow this must be a concern for every Catholic. After all, our vision of heaven is all the followers of Christ gathered around the Lamb as a great Communion of Saints. This includes the membership of the churches and ecclesial communities with whom we currently are separated.

The pastoral plan I mentioned earlier, *Go and Make Disciples*, outlines numerous possible approaches to evangelization. Each faith community must look at itself and its resources to determine what is most effective. (By faith community, I include units such as faith-filled families, small Christian communities, prayer groups, and intentional communities, as well as parishes.) In general, these faith communities ought to strive to accomplish the three main goals of the pastoral plan:

- Faith communities should create a sufficient level of enthusiasm in each of their members so that the faith of their members will be lived in a day-to-day manner. Filled with such enthusiasm for the Lord, the members will freely desire to share Christ with others.
- Every faith community should provide a welcoming and hospitable atmosphere and embody a genuine concern for the temporal and spiritual well-being of all people. Parishes in particular should be places where people who search for meaning and purpose, whatever their social condition or cultural background, are invited to hear the message of salvation in Christ.
- Faith communities should instill gospel values in the society of which they are a part, promoting the dignity of the human person, advancing the importance of the family, and advocating for the common good.

Conclusion

In order for a faith community to carry out its mission effectively, a significant proportion of its membership must be involved. Baptized into Christ and confirmed in the Spirit of Jesus, we become members of his Eucharistic Body. As a Eucharistic Body of Christ, we ourselves are bread to be broken and shared for the world; we ourselves are precious droplets of his blood to be poured out for others. What we do with the hours of our day, how we use the abilities with which we have been blessed, and how we utilize the material resources over which we have responsibility expresses how well or how poorly we understand ourselves as a Eucharistic Body. Without a true sense of spiritual stewardship over how we use our time and energies, and without a significant proportion of the Church's membership, the mission of the Church can and does become ineffective. While a small group of individuals can have a tremendous effect (or even one person, as is illustrated in the lives of many great saints), it is more profound and fruitful when the entire faith community is involved.

The spirituality of stewardship is important because it provides the means for the Church to be an effective witness of Christ and his Gospel in our world. We are formed as disciples so that we may be sent as apostles. A disciple is one who follows, who patterns his or her life on the life of a Master. In the case of Christianity, the Master is the Risen Lord. An apostle is one who is sent. As a part of an apostolic Church, each of us shares in some way the responsibility to bring Christ "to the ends of the earth." Stewardship provides the time, energy, and resources to make the essential mission of the Church possible.

How do we get this message across? I would like to offer an approach that includes ongoing conversion and continuing Christian formation. Parish leaders—such as the pastor and his staff, pastoral council, finance council, various parish committees, as well as each individual member—need to evaluate regularly their lifestyle choices in light of the dominant values found in secular culture. Rather than fall prey to the influence of consumerism, individualism, and materialism, an honest attempt must be made to cultivate gospel values and beliefs, especially those that reflect charity, justice, and peace. Likewise, a deep devotional life needs to be fostered and promoted both individually and communally. Opportunities for contemplation and adoration need to be a part of any faith community's regular spiritual routine. Worship is vital and at the heart of our faith experience. Worship, however, must be more than just doing the rubric right. Worship must be heartfelt, the kind that moves God's people into action. People need real contact with God. Real connections must be made with what is taking place at worship and what is occurring in people's day-to-day activity. As such, parish worship needs to touch not only the mind but also the heart. Members of the Church need to have opportunities for days for prayer, retreats, and spiritual direction. The point is to lead people not only to full, conscious, and active participation at worship, but to a life that is alive in Christ, conscious of the presence of his Spirit and responding actively to opportunities to serve God at all times. As members of the Church assume responsibility for their spiritual relationship with God in Christ, they will look seriously at their lifestyle choices: how they use their material resources, how they expend their energies, how they spend their time. When people honestly desire to respond to the Gospel, they try to make choices that reflect it.

Unless we actively use our gifts, it doesn't matter how many talents we have or how wealthy or important we seem to be, for our gifts will remain useless. God has blessed us with whatever we have so that we might use these gifts for God's purposes and design. Ultimately, this means we use them to share our faith.

Catholic men (and here I refer mostly to laity) have a responsibility to share in the Church's mission of proclaiming salvation in Christ. Too often, this responsibility has been left solely to others. However, when Catholic men have assumed this role, they have made a definite impact in the world around them. It is my prayer that the movement of the Spirit that has caused Catholic men to embrace their faith vibrantly will continue to flourish and spread throughout the land. ∎

Bishop Michael W. Warfel *was ordained in 1996 as the fourth Bishop of the Diocese of Juneau, Alaska, and serves currently as Chairman of the United States Conference of Catholic Bishops' Committee on Evangelization.*

SUGGESTED FURTHER READING FROM THE VATICAN AND BISHOPS' CONFERENCE

Vatican: *Evangelii Nuntiandi* (*On Evangelization in the Modern World*); *Gospel of Life* (*Evangelium Vitae*)

U.S. Catholic Bishops: *Because We Are Disciples* (video); *Called to Global Solidarity*; *Church Without Borders* (video); *Go and Make Disciples: A National Plan and Strategy for Catholic Evangelization in the United States*; *Here I Am, Send Me: A Conference Response to the Evangelization of African Americans*; *The Hispanic Presence in the New Evangelization in the United States*; *A Time to Listen . . . A Time to Heal*

See p. 92 for ordering information.

Men with Other Men: Building an Inclusive Ministry

BY BISHOP GABINO ZAVALA

In every age humankind has searched and struggled to find a symbol that articulates adequately the condition of its era. In this age of modern technology, we'd be hard-pressed to name one that isn't immediately outdated. In my effort to reflect on a symbol that would speak to the reality of the diversity that defines our society and Church, I rejected those of a time long past: the "melting pot" and the often referred-to substitute, the "salad bowl." I remembered as a child having a simple gadget that entertained and held the attention of my playmates and me. That toy was the kaleidoscope. I realize that I'm not here to talk about toys. But it is a symbol that guided my reflections through the Encuentro 2000 process, and I offer it to you as we look at inclusivity and ministry through Encuentro lenses.

The Symbol of the Kaleidoscope

How many of you recall the kaleidoscope? It is a tubular object. At one end, you have many pieces of differently shaped, sized, and colored glass or plastic. This end is covered by a sheath of opaque material that allows a measure of light to pass through. This part of the kaleidoscope also twists, making it possible to configure and reconfigure a multitude of colorful designs. The other end of the tube has a small hole cut into it, allowing us to see through the body of the tube and catch a glimpse of the designs. The amount of light filtered through affects the clarity and brilliance of each design.

The kaleidoscope captures both light and shadow and brings them together harmoniously to reflect the whole. No matter how you shake, toss, or twist it, you always end up with an inclusive and wondrous design. In the kaleidoscope the pieces always fit. They are asymmetrical. No matter if the shapes are odd or diverse, they come together to make the whole.

The kaleidoscope reminds me that unity in diversity is at the heart of God's design for all humankind, that all belong and have a rightful place; no one or any part of God's creation is to be excluded. We are to welcome and embrace all of God's own, especially the poor, weak, marginalized, and differently abled. If any piece is missing, the design is incomplete. In using Encuentro 2000 language, we would say that "there are many faces, 'many rooms,' in God's house."

The kaleidoscope speaks to the reality that, at times, we need to be shaken from our comfort zones to expand our horizons: a fact that we can no longer ignore when considering the events of the last few months. It tells us that our shadow sides cannot be ignored either, but that we must bring these parts of our lives, culture, and society into the light, God's light. The Encuentro 2000 process invited us to be enlightened by the experience of another; to be stretched, touched, and moved by their story; to readopt the Gospel as our tool for assessment, our standard for judgment. Like the symbol of the kaleidoscope, the Encuentro 2000 process called us to reconfigure ourselves so as to be in a position to embrace the otherwise unknown or perhaps unwelcome, to see those different from ourselves as part of what makes us whole and our world complete. Encuentro 2000 invited us to enter into the experience of metanoia: a change of heart that may call for a turning or twisting, that allows us to create a new space in our lives for that which is of God, and that allows us to turn away from anything that is not of God, so as to be a "piece" that lends harmony to the design God has for creation.

Through a process that involved profound conversations, Encuentro 2000 called all to conversion, communion, and solidarity—elements that will prove to be constitutive in laying the foundation for building an inclusive ministry. The response to this invitation was structured in a way that provided focus sessions. Each session included the following:

- Communal prayer
- Shared stories and experiences in an atmosphere where they could be heard and respected
- A dialogue prompted by prepared questions on the focus of a particular session and shared experiences or stories
- Input in the form of a presentation that reflected on our faith tradition in light of the topic
- Time to formulate a concrete and appropriate response to what had transpired in the context of putting our faith into action
- An "evaluation" of the process: what took place that was helpful and true to our purposes and what adjustments needed to be made
- An opportunity to give thanks and to celebrate the God who is present to and with the community that was gathered

Individuals were trained to facilitate the process. Guidelines for interaction were agreed upon. Also, a process for "sharing" dialogue and formulating conclusions was established. The guiding principles were based on and taken from Eric Law's Mutual Invitation Process and respectful communication guidelines. They were intended to create an environment of mutual support and receptivity, one where confidences were held and in which a person felt safe to engage in appropriate self-disclosure.

The Encuentro Process and Dialogue

In planning this process we drew on what we learned from what has been coined as "the New Evangelization." Faith must be in dialogue with life, people, cultures, and systems. Evangelization grasps and recognizes the God who acts and interacts with a people and does so within their social, cultural, and religious context. Promoting and participating in the mission of Jesus is the prerogative and responsibility of all the baptized. Human dignity and the fullness of life for all is first and foremost a function of evangelization—hence, the struggle for justice, the liberation of peoples, and the "transformation" or reordering of the world is the priority. And public witness is no longer an option; rather it is essential to being Christian, a disciple. This transformation is the path to salvation. In light of this we were reminded that any process needed to include

- An attentiveness to the signs of the times
- A regard for the symbols that convey meaning to a particular people

- A listening to and the incorporation of the stories and traditions that sustain a peoples' faith and support its expression
- An invitation to move beyond one's personal or communal boundaries
- A re-introduction to the truth that all the baptized are called to be bearers of the Good News

We invited people to hear the Word in light of their own experiences and the experiences of others, in a gathering that reflected the layers and complexity of the diversity that characterizes our Church and society. We asked people to bring with them and share with us the symbols that so enrich and energize their faith life. We admitted our corporate failures and looked at ways that they could be redressed today. We proclaimed that we are one people, the people of God. And, in doing so, we acknowledged that what affects one of us affects all of us; we must act so that no one person, group, or nation is adversely affected or denied what rightly is theirs as children of God. We gave praise and thanks, in a myriad of expressions, to the God who has blessed us in so many ways and who loves us beyond our comprehension and calls us to love one another in the same way.

The sharing of stories seemed to be the aspect of the Encuentro process that had the most profound and lasting effect. Both those told in the general sessions and those shared in the small groups touched many deeply. Relationships were forged, and the sharing of stories proved to be the segue to entering into profound conversation. Our stance of respectful listening and openness enabled us to make new discoveries. People had names, characteristics, qualities, and gifts. Groups had different customs and traditions, but all embraced and celebrated core values and beliefs. We spoke different languages but were able to communicate. Stereotypes were dispelled and myths dismissed, for these profound conversations allowed us to know one another, not just to know about each other. They bound us in a way that we never would have imagined. It was humbling to listen to the struggles of others; painful to be told of their suffering or loss; exciting to be privy to their hopes and dreams; interesting to discover the meaning of certain rituals, the importance of a symbol, or the significance of a special feast; a privilege to share another's experience of God. These profound conversations enabled us to learn, broaden our horizons, and expand our worlds—to let go of the burden that ignorance or prejudice of necessity brings. They afforded us opportunities to sympathize, empathize, or identify with another. Through them we gained insight and wisdom, new and unique lenses through which our world view was changed. We were able to see in another the face of God, and a little more of the Kingdom was revealed.

To engage in this level of conversation required the participants to be constructive and skilled. It required the commitment to be constructive, to work at building up and strengthening relationships. It involved the cultivating of gospel attitudes and values, including the following: a profound regard for the human person, a respect for the individual and their experience, an appreciation for diversity, a presumption of good will on the part of the other, the ability to acknowledge one's own truth and to receive the truth of another, an openness to forge the bonds of trust, a belief in the power of conversion, and a desire to meet God in the other. The skills we needed to cultivate were those that fostered dialogue.

We needed to be able to listen and to engage in active listening, to be fully present and attentive to the person—not only hearing the words spoken but also the emotion conveyed, perceptions communicated, and the body language displayed. We had to set aside our ideas, keep reactions in check, and hold thoughts in abeyance, so as not to interrupt or give unsolicited advice. To listen in this fashion called for the suspension of judgment, to put oneself in a place in order to understand what the other is saying or feeling. It also challenged us to find a way to communicate our comprehension and acceptance.

Dialogue involves active listening and fosters mutuality, thus enabling us to engage in profound or in-depth conversations. It promotes unity and fosters solidarity. For to be effective, we must be aware of our own communication style or patterns and be open to allowing ourselves to be influenced by another; we must desire to converse in an open and honest fashion, to own and be responsible for what is said; and we must be truly willing to listen and learn, to be able to keep confidences when asked or when appropriate. We must also be able to articulate our own truth and experience and to draw on them. None of us possesses the whole truth; we each have a piece that leads to the whole . . . to unity.

Dialogue allows for and respects difference of opinions or views. It refrains from labeling and making assumptions or presumptions. It trusts in the good faith of the participants and frees one to explore the space or world of another.

Encuentro 2000: Inclusion, Solidarity, Conversion, Communion

Encuentro 2000 was about hospitality and inclusion. All were welcome and all came. The gatherings were intercultural, interethnic, interracial, and intergenerational. Men and women with all kinds of abilities, sensibilities, and vulnerabilities participated. They brought their different personalities, histories and experiences, and senses and ways of being Church. Faith and its tradition provided a common ground for interaction, for at the heart of the matter all acknowledged that we were children of the same God, brothers and sisters to one another, deserving of dignity and respect. Though our differences were many, we were one: one by virtue of a common "Father," a shared belief, gospel convictions, the need to be in relationship, the desire to move beyond self, and an acknowledgement that we have responsibilities for the state of the world, the order of the universe. Encuentro 2000 was also about conversion, communion, and solidarity. This invitation was issued to all levels of life: personal, communal, ecclesial, and indeed global. We took our "lead" from Pope John Paul II, who asked us to usher in the new millennium as the "New Jerusalem," an era in which we were reconciled to self, God, one another, the earth, and all creation, so that we might be people of one heart, soul, and mind, that we might be those who have found unity and salvation in the one God.

Our Holy Father called us to live in solidarity—brother and sister to each living being:
- Thinking of, feeling with, and caring for each one as we would our own biological family
- Sharing what we have with those in need, not out of our excess but from our substance
- Being uncomfortable with the growing gap between the rich and poor

- Using our voices, influence, and networks to dismantle systems that diminish human life and dignity
- Rejecting the "isms" that isolate, denigrate, or exclude—that reduce persons to objects
- Not tolerating violence in any form

This is part of what it means to live in solidarity, to live as "just" men in the eyes of God. Solidarity enables us to experience our dependence on God and our interdependence with all creatures and creation. It defies the imbalance we now experience with the distribution of the world's goods and resources and with opportunities for employment, health care, and housing. If we truly desire to be in communion, solidarity is an attitude we must embrace and a stance we must take.

In order to accept this call to solidarity we must enter the process of conversion—a process because it is forever ongoing! As individuals we strive for that metanoia, or change of heart, that directs our way of being to God. We desire and strive to be in right relationship with self, God, God's people, and creation. This means letting go of any beliefs, attitudes, or behaviors that would have us fall short of living fully the great commandment of love. Society, local and global, must also enter into the process of conversion, rejecting all that is not of God and re-ordering systems so as to reflect the highest regard for humanity and the harmony God intended for the universe. Accepting stewardship over creation, and the responsibility to guard and protect our natural environment and to treasure and use wisely its resources, is also inherent to the process of conversion. The Church is called to conversion, to ensure that its public witness and pastoral practice indeed proclaim the Good News and serve to make the Kingdom present.

Communion is not a state but a way of being in relationship. It is inclusive and interactive; it reflects God's desire for us and God's plan for creation. Communion is about "at-oneness." We are called to be one with our Triune God, one with our brothers and sisters, one in harmony with all creatures and creation. In communion we discover that all have a rightful place and each one of us reveals the face of God. Together we are the revelation of God. In communion we make the Body of Christ whole and functioning properly. If anyone is left out, God will not be revealed fully—the Kingdom will not come.

Building an Inclusive Men's Ministry
So what does all this have to do with men and building an inclusive ministry? Actually, quite a lot. First and foremost, we need to recognize that diversity exists and calls us to integrity, acknowledging that without this diversity we are incomplete. From the onset, a concerted effort should be made to invite men who reflect the many faces of God. In your ministry with men should be men of every color, race, language, and culture as reflected in our Church here in the United States. There should be men from urban backgrounds, inner cities, suburbs, and rural America. We should represent men of every age and economic bracket. Hospitality should be primary since it plays a vital role in creating an environment where all are comfortable and feel welcome to participate.

From Encuentro 2000 we learned that a consistent structure was helpful in keeping us focused and served to enable participation. In developing our process, we adapted the see-judge-act methodology, which is popular in the Hispanic community. Basically, it was a process of theological reflection, of which there are many forms to choose. This methodology brings faith and life into dialogue. It invites its participants to reflect prayerfully on their lived experience in light of gospel teaching and values and to listen to where God might be leading and calling them, personally or as a community. Theological reflection respects our different personal situations, the uncertainty of the times, the complex moral questions and ethical concerns we face, as well as our struggles with the Church or her teachings. It gives us permission to use stories, to draw on tradition, and to introduce symbols. Theological reflection calls us beyond our universe and ourselves. It acknowledges that God is to be found everywhere: in persons, in situations, in the environment.

Integral to this process is the articulation of one's story and the active listening to another's. Some men may find this difficult, but it is essential that we help one another hone the skills to do so. Finding a voice to articulate some of my recent experiences has been a blessing. So much seems to fall into perspective. The reflections of others have lent me support and guidance and served to reinforce my conviction. It has also been good to know that I have companions on this journey in faith and in being faithful to the struggle.

Spirituality in this context is the lived experience of one's relationship with God, God's people, and creation. It is an inclusive spirituality that calls us to pray and to act. It is done in the context of community, thus broadening our worlds. I have found that in this setting, no matter how personal the sharing, I'm called outside of myself. The strengthening of relationships, though, is its best byproduct.

Establishing guidelines for interaction and using the mutual invitation process helped to create a free and safe environment. Knowing that what was said in the group stayed there was as important as knowing that you could speak when and if you felt ready. It is a way to recognize the God within each person and to demonstrate respect for the person.

Clearly articulated purposes ensure faithfulness to the endeavor and will provide an appropriate starting point for any evaluation. The input from assessment allows for adjustments that will better enable us to meet the established goals. The goals and objectives of necessity must reflect our universal nature, gospel values, and Catholic social justice principles. The structure and content should emerge from the identified and articulated needs, as well as those inherent to our faith traditions. They should allow for a wide scope of interests and expressions and cannot be divorced from the world around us or isolated and confined to the individual or local group.

We also learned through all the preparations that some people were not ready for this type of interaction, this in-depth conversation. The same may be true with regard to an inclusive ministry for men; however, we must say, it was and is time for such a venture. Men need a forum to build honest, strong, and companionable relationships—relationships that welcome and include all. We need a structure to guide us and the skills that enable us to participate fully. We need to identify issues, talk about our particular concerns, and reflect on our questions in light of our faith traditions. We need a venue to focus the energy we have for good, for revealing God's face, and for making a difference in the world. We are part of what makes communion and are essential to a world called to live in solidarity.

Conclusion

So let's take another look at the kaleidoscope. Let's look through that small hole in the lens with new eyes and see what possibilities lie ahead for us if we allow ourselves to be shaken and twisted, to be configured or reconfigured, in a design that creates an inclusive ministry for men with men. I am confident that what emerges will facilitate the revelation of the face of God and bring about God's kingdom in this age, that it will reflect and encompass God's design for the universe. ∎

Bishop Gabino Zavala *is an Auxiliary Bishop of the Archdiocese of Los Angeles. He serves currently on the United States Conference of Catholic Bishops' committees for Laity, Priestly Formation, Hispanic Affairs, Canonical Affairs, Education, and Evangelization, and on the Bishops' Editorial Oversight Board for the* National Adult Catechism.

SUGGESTED FURTHER READING FROM THE
VATICAN AND BISHOPS' CONFERENCE

Vatican: *Ecclesia in America* (*The Church in America*)

U.S. Catholic Bishops: *Brothers and Sisters to Us/Nuestros Hermanos y Hermanas; Circle of the Spirit* (video); *Follow the Way of Love: A Pastoral Message of the U.S. Catholic Bishops to Families; Hispanic Ministry: Three Major Documents; Love Thy Neighbor as Thyself: U.S. Catholic Bishops Speak Against Racism; Many Faces in God's House* (various); *Sharing Faith Across the Hemisphere; Strangers and Aliens No More; Welcoming the Stranger Among Us* (various); *Who Are My Sisters and Brothers* (various)

See p. 92 for ordering information.

Key Biblical Passages for Constructing Male Spiritual Insights

BY REV. LAWRENCE BOADT, CSP

The following are important texts for penetrating the relationship between God and humanity, between the Holy One of the Covenant and the chosen people of Israel, between Jesus and his disciples. These texts have much to say about the themes of male spirituality. The selections are not exhaustive, but men may find them fruitful for developing as responsible members of the Church and becoming more in tune with the ideal of the true Israelite, the faithful disciple of Jesus.

Samples from Genesis

Genesis 1	The purpose of God in Creation
Genesis 12	Abraham has the courage to answer a call to a new life
Genesis 15	Abraham's struggle to know God's will despite doubt and fear
Genesis 22	The sacrifice of Isaac and the poignancy of a father's love
Genesis 32:22-32	How Jacob wrestles with God in a partnership
Genesis 33	Jacob knows how to seek forgiveness from his brother Esau
Genesis 37, 45	Joseph's transformation from self-centered to altruistic

Old Testament Texts from the Pentateuch

Exodus 4-6	Moses's struggle to answer his mission without losing heart
Exodus 33-34	The intimate friendship between Moses and God

Leviticus 19	Dutiful laws of neighborly love in imitation of God
Deuteronomy 4	A wonderful theology of finding God in difficult times
Deuteronomy 6	The divine commandment of love for a people of loyalty
Deuteronomy 8-9	The challenge of doing good, rejecting evil for God's blessing
Deuteronomy 30	The great choice given to each person to follow God or not

Texts from the Historical Books

Judges 3:12-30	The Judge Ehud and his courage and cleverness
Ruth 3-4	The nobility of Boaz as a model Israelite
1 Samuel 3	The story of Samuel's call to serve God in his youth
1 Samuel 12	Samuel's defense of his life of service to God
1 Samuel 24	David spares the life of Saul out of fidelity and generosity
2 Samuel 9	David's generosity to the family of Saul
2 Samuel 18-19	David shows a father's grief over the death of his son Absalom
1 Kings 3	The wisdom and humility of Solomon
1 Kings 19	Elijah in his desolation and emptiness seeks God
1 Kings 21	Elijah and his sense of justice over Naboth's vineyard
1 Kings 22	The strength of Micaiah to stand alone in his convictions
2 Kings 18-19	The prophet Isaiah and King Hezekiah show deep trust in God

Texts from the Prophets

Isaiah 38	The prayer of trust of Hezekiah
Isaiah 42:1-6	The description of the ideal servant of God
Isaiah 50:4-9	The suffering of the servant who is faithful
Jeremiah 12	The prayer of Jeremiah in persecution
Jeremiah 20:7-18	Jeremiah's interior crisis and prayer to God
Jeremiah 32	Jeremiah's courageous risk with his money in wartime
Ezekiel 3-5	The hardships of Ezekiel to convince his people of danger
Daniel 2	Daniel's bravery in interpreting Nebuchadnezzar's dream
Daniel 3	The courage of the three friends of Daniel in the fiery furnace
Daniel 6	Daniel's courage and faith in the lion's den
Hosea 1-3	The story of Hosea's marriage
Amos 7	Amos undertakes a difficult and opposed mission
Habakkuk 1-2	A man of faith in terrible times

Other Old Testament Writings

Job 1-2	The story of a just man named Job
Tobit 1-2	The story of a faithful and upright follower of the faith
Sirach 25-26	The description of a man of wisdom in society
2 Chronicles 20	King Jehoshaphat as a model of royal obedience to God
Nehemiah 2, 5	The story of Nehemiah as an outstanding man of integrity
1 Maccabees 2	The story of Mattathias

Some Important Gospel Texts

Matthew 5:1-12	The Beatitudes
Matthew 6:9-13	The Our Father
Matthew 6:25-34	The lilies of the field
Matthew 11:25-27	The lesson of children
Mark 2:1-12	The healing of the paralyzed
Mark 7:14-23	The things that defile from within
Mark 10:17-31	The conditions for membership in the Kingdom
Luke 15:11-32	The prodigal son
Luke 18:9-14	The publican and the Pharisee
Luke 24:13-35	The Emmaus story
John 10:1-18	The good shepherd
John 17:1-26	Jesus' prayer for his disciples

The Acts of the Apostles

Acts 2-5	Peter as the leader of the Church and his leadership charisma
Acts 6-7	The story of Stephen, the first martyr
Acts 13	Paul explains his ministry and conversion
Acts 16:1-5	Timothy is called by Paul
Acts 18:1-11	Timothy as Paul's trusted envoy

The Letters of Paul

Romans 8	Paul's description of our life in the Spirit
1 Corinthians 13	The power of love
Philippians 2:5-11	The emptying of Jesus for us
Ephesians 3:14-21	Paul's prayer for the Church
Ephesians 5:21-33	Paul's household codes
Colossians 1:15-20	Christ as our head
1 and 2 Timothy	Paul describes the ideal disciple as Timothy

Catholic Men's Ministry: Beginning a Parish-Based Group

What Are Catholic Men's Groups?
Catholic men's groups are gatherings of men—usually from the same parish—who come together regularly to discuss their lives in the light of their Catholic faith and to share this faith through friendship, prayer, and action. Groups can be any size but typically include six to fifteen men. Members support one another and share insights about the difficulties men encounter both in their families and in their work. They seek God's help in dealing with issues they confront every day. Members strive to reinforce Christian values in their home, share those values with others in the group, and support those struggling to do the same.

Men who regularly participate in a group cultivate friendships among fellow parishioners, have fun, and learn from each other about how to be a better husband, father, son, employee, Christian man, and Catholic parishioner. Many men say they have grown by this experience, which has helped them to form stronger and happier families and to cope better with the stresses they encounter at work.

Groups meet typically for ninety minutes twice a month, on the same day, at the same time, to pray and study Scripture, Catholic doctrine, or Catholic male spirituality. The purpose of these gatherings is to foster spiritual growth for men in the parish. For example, in the mission statement for the Southeastern Wisconsin Catholic Men's Ministry, this is called "helping Catholic men to learn to walk as Godly men."

Does a Catholic Men's Group Need a Leader or Facilitator?

A facilitator is of great value in leading a group. He need not be an expert in church doctrine or Scripture, though some knowledge of both would be helpful. A facilitator does not function as a teacher. His primary responsibilities are to keep the group focused on the particular subject, to ensure that each one in the group has the chance to participate, and to keep the discussion moving.

If the group is new, it is best for one person to serve as facilitator. After the group has bonded and the men have become comfortable with each other, the facilitator's role may be rotated among the members who are interested in leading the process. This will prepare men to lead another group when the current group grows beyond eight or ten members.

What's in It for the Parish?

As Catholic men in the parish grow in the depth and richness of their Catholic faith, they may become more active as liturgical ministers, liturgy committee members, or outreach volunteers. Often they experience a hunger for God's word and a desire to share it with Christian formation, youth ministry, and/or adult education programs. Men involved with Catholic men's groups can be expected to seek out leadership roles on the parish council and its affiliated committees.

How Do You Get Started?

The National Resource Center for Catholic Men (*www.nrccm.org*) offers a *Starter's Kit for Catholic Men's Groups* as well as other resources and ideas. Their website contains a listing of regional and diocesan Catholic men's ministry organizations. If one already exists in your diocese or area, then you might want to affiliate your parish group with this larger structure. If not, then the center can still offer you help in starting anew.

Above all, don't be afraid to take first steps in forming genuine relationships with other men. You will be surprised at how much your faith will be strengthened and how you will grow in your roles as husband, father, and disciple of Jesus Christ by being part of a group of Catholic men who love the Lord and desire to serve him as well as one another.

The pastor, parish director, pastoral associate, or parish leader may have been thinking about men's ministry in the parish and its potential benefits. Men in your parish may have already approached the parish leader about starting a group. The leader's own experience will confirm that spirituality cannot be imposed; rather, men will respond out of a personal invitation and will not thrive unless they have a spiritual center and a continuing spiritual focus. The decision to form a men's group should be made only after the parish has prayerfully considered it and has asked the parish men to do the same. Consider also that a men's group in the parish demands commitment from parish leadership as well as the men's group participants.

What Does the Parish Need to Do?
- *Select a Spiritual Advisor.* The pastor, parish director, pastoral associate, or parish leader will want to consider how to support the group. A men's group needs a spiritual advisor and encouragement from a significant Catholic role model in the parish. A parish leader would be the first choice to fill that role, but someone else—a qualified Catholic appointed by a leader—would also be suitable.
- *Appoint a Group Leader.* Central to success for all groups is that they stay focused on matters of Scripture, Catholic doctrine, and/or Catholic male spirituality. The group will need a leader who is selected by the group to keep things spiritually centered from meeting to meeting. Initially the parish leader may want to ask a man who has spiritual leadership tendencies to take the role. It is best if the group leader is not also the spiritual advisor.
- *Decide on a Gathering Location.* The parish will need to decide on the gathering location for its men's group, as most men's groups meet at a parish facility. The gathering spot should be welcoming and conducive to prayer. Space should also be available in the event that the large gathering breaks into smaller discussion groups.
- *Get Help.* As the parish men discern the decision to start a Catholic men's group, contact a vital men's group in your area to explore resources via a men's ministry website such as *www.catholicmensresurces.org*.

What Are the Logistics of Beginning a Group?
- Choose a meeting location.
- Choose an initial meeting date and time, and future meeting schedule.

- Publicize the first meeting.
- Invite a mentor parish representative, that is, someone from an active men's group in the area.
- Select and obtain study materials.
- Determine the format for the group.
- Assign readings.
- Arrange for refreshments.
- Determine meeting format.

This article is based on information submitted by Randy Nohl of the Southeastern Wisconsin Catholic Men's Ministry.

SAMPLE FORMAT FOR MEN'S MINISTRY GROUP

First and third Saturdays of each month from 7:30-9:00 A.M.

Opening Song
A theme song and 2-3 others are sung.

Praise
The men are led in a quiet expression of praise to the Lord.

Spontaneous Witness
Members describe the Lord's action in their lives through work, family, and friends, as well as answers to prayer.

Prayer and Special Intercessions
All are encouraged to express praise, glory, and gratitude to the Lord and/or request intercession for their needs and concerns.

Scripture
Short passages in support of the discussion theme are read by different men; comments on the readings are encouraged.

Discussion
Comments are "drawn out" relating to the theme.

Business

A brief time is alloted for announcements or other business.

Closing Prayer

A "summary" prayer, if appropriate, and the Lord's Prayer close the meeting.

Complementary Plans

- Celebrate Mass during the year, e.g., during Christmas and Easter.
- Conduct a reconciliation service on a regular basis.
- Look for other resources such as tapes and live speakers.
- Plan fifth Saturday programs around wives and families.
- Organize a prayer chain.

SAMPLE OPERATING PRINCIPLES

- Spread out preparatory work.
- Use one or two facilitators to maintain a standard.
- Plan with a 3-6 member leadership team that is co-responsible and non-hierarchical.
- Pre-plan each meeting, but be flexible, responsive, and able to adjust to an individual's needs.
- Establish a predictable and comfortable format that fosters spontaneity.
- Start with a few "social" moments, and stop on time.
- Develop a small-group (5-7 men) infrastructure that ties in with large group.
- Position the large group as the "tool" for evangelization, the vehicle for attracting men to the fellowship.
- Initiate a weekend retreat during the large group's start-up phase and on an annual basis thereafter.
- Organize the large-group meeting in a circle so that each man's "ritual space" is respected.
- Encourage personal witnessing and "testimonies" to build faith.
- Do not establish "rules and regulations."
- Meet the men "where they are" and avoid making demands.
- Keep brief reference notes on each meeting and maintain a resource "library."

This text is based on the format and operating principles used by the Catholic Men's Fellowship of Greater Cincinnati.

To order the resources suggested in this book or other USCCB documents, please call 800-235-8722 or check out the U.S. Catholic bishops' website at *www.usccb.org.*